The Bible
AND THE HUMAN MIND
J.C. METCALFE

CHRISTIAN • LITERATURE • CRUSADE
Fort Washington, Pennsylvania 19034

CHRISTIAN LITERATURE CRUSADE

U.S.A.
P.O. Box 1449, Fort Washington, PA 19034

GREAT BRITAIN
51 The Dean, Alresford, Hants., SO24 9BJ

AUSTRALIA
P.O. Box 91, Pennant Hills, N.S.W. 2120

NEW ZEALAND
10 MacArthur Street, Feilding

ISBN 0-87508-913-5

First American Edition
(Contemporized)
1995

ALL RIGHTS RESERVED. No part of this publication may be translated, reproduced or transmitted in any form or by any means, electronic or mechanical, including photocopy, recording, or any information storage and retrieval system, without permission in writing from the publisher.

PRINTED IN THE UNITED STATES OF AMERICA

CONTENTS

Chapter	Page
1. The Scope of Our Study	7
2. The Mind	13
3. Thoughts	29
4. The Balancing of Ideas	37
5. The Intellect	45
6. Understanding	53
7. Full Understanding	63
8. Reflection	73
9. Practical Wisdom	77
10. Mind and Emotion	89
11. The Mind Produces an Attitude	95
12. The Mind Produces a Purpose	101
13. Conscience	107
14. Soul and Spirit	117
15. The Heart	125
Appendix—list of verbs related to the nouns studied in these chapters.	135

THE GREEK ALPHABET

Capital Letters	Small Letters	Name	Transliteration and Pronunciation
Α	α	*al'pha*	a
Β	β	*bē'ta*	b
Γ	γ	*gam'ma*	g hard, as in be*g*in[1]
Δ	δ	*děl'ta*	d
Ε	ε	*ě'psi·lŏn*	e short, as in m*e*t
Ζ	ζ	*zē'ta*	z
Η	η	*ē'ta*	e long, as in th*ey*
Θ	θ	*thē'ta*	th
Ι	ι	*i·ō'ta*	i as in ma*ch*ine
Κ	κ	*kap'pa*	k
Λ	λ	*lam'bda*	l
Μ	μ	*my*	m
Ν	ν	*ny*	n
Ξ	ξ	*xi*	x
Ο	ο	*ŏ'mi·krŏn*	o short, as in l*o*t
Π	π	*pi*	p
Ρ	ρ	*hrō*	r
Σ	σ, ς (final)	*sig'ma*	s
Τ	τ	*tau*	t
Υ	υ	*y'psi·lŏn*	y[2] French u or German ü
Φ	φ	*phi*	ph as in *ph*ase
Χ	χ	*khi*	kh as in el*kh*orn
Ψ	ψ	*psi*	ps as in li*ps*
Ω	ω	*ō·mě'ga*	o long, as in n*o*te

᾿ is silent while ῾ is pronounced like an *h*

[1] Except before κ, ξ, χ, or another γ when it is pronounced nasal, like *ng* in a*ng*er

[2] υ is *u* in diphthongs

Note: Modern Greek pronunciation varies from the above.

CHAPTER 1

THE SCOPE OF OUR STUDY

OVER recent years much research has been carried out in the realm of the mind. Psychology has therefore come to be regarded as supplying a means of guiding our youth into the walk of life best suited to their ability and temperament, and is called upon to play an important part in dealing with the mental maladjustments which seem increasingly to be by-products of the stress and strain of modern life. In the realm of religion it is now no uncommon thing for the principles of psychoanalysis to be applied in an attempt to iron out some of the personal problems that mar church life. Discoveries of a more sinister nature have also been made, and used ruthlessly, in modern totalitarian political systems, by means of which a man's whole mental approach to life can be twisted out of all recognition and confessions extorted from him about matters quite outside his knowledge.

The New Testament has much to say about the mind in its varying aspects, and I have sought to collect some of its teachings and place them side by side in order to simplify their study. To this end various Greek nouns dealing with the mind, its attributes and its workings, have been brought together in a manner designed to give information which may prove to be of particular value to those who are seeking to win men for Christ and establish them in the faith. I have proceeded on the assumption that the Scriptures provide us with every bit of knowledge and equipment we can possibly need for this task, if we will dig deeply enough to find it.

The grand objective of the gospel of Jesus Christ *is nothing less than the building up of a new creation in Him.* The only place where we can learn anything of this "new creation" is the Bible, where God lays down His own explanation of the need for and the workings of this miracle of grace. For this reason I have deliberately avoided approaching our study from the angle of secular psychological teaching, and only sought to gather up the main lines of Scriptural revelation.

This is *not* an exhaustive study. I have already been asked, for instance—"Why leave out the verbs and concentrate on the nouns?" The answer seems to me to be that the verbs merely tell the same story; and I have included at the back of the book a list of those having the same root as the nouns viewed in these pages, so that any who wish to carry our study further may do so for themselves.

I have gone through a good deal of heart-searching about the method of handling the available material which I have employed. I have wondered whether this straightforward plowing through the necessary passages of Scripture with comparatively brief comments might frighten some intending readers. This is, however, for better or for worse, my own style of working, and I feel I can do no other! Also I am anxious not to make propositions and then quote texts to back up my contentions. The Bible is our sole authority in matters relating to God's dealings with man, and it is surely our business to first find out what is said and then to seek to put what we have found into practice in our daily living.

The necessity for the intimate union of knowledge and life, and of mind with heart, is something that has been borne in upon me irresistibly as I have studied. Oswald Chambers in his book *Biblical Psychology* says: "The heart is the appointed place of meeting not only for all the life of the body physically but for all the life of the soul and spirit. . . . The Bible places in the heart what modern science puts in the brain." I also saw recently that a noted psychologist was reported as saying that the heart is our inner consciousness, where the thoughts, affections and will all meet. I have therefore added two chapters dealing respectively with the heart and the conscience, as well as a brief memorandum on the distinction between soul and spirit and the relationship of all these to our study. The well-integrated development of the whole inner man is of great importance in the Christian life.

To return to the mind—J. A. James in his book *The Anxious Enquirer* underlines the necessity for a clear mental grasp of truth as the only basis upon which a healthy spiritual life can be founded. He says: "It is important that you should perceive that the whole superstructure of personal godliness rests upon knowledge. True conversion is emphatically called *coming to a knowledge of the truth*. . . . The reason why so many turn back and others go on so slowly is because they do not study to make themselves acquainted with divine truth."

Having acknowledged the accuracy of

The Scope of Our Study / 11

this statement, we must finally note two opposite trends of overbalance against which we need to be on our guard. The first is the danger of minimizing the value of an active, enquiring mind in the Christian life, and therefore of drifting, through sheer ignorance, into passive impressions, which can open the door to many dire perils. The second is to miss the fact that the human mind can never grasp divine truth apart from the teaching of the Holy Spirit of God, who indwells every born-again Christian, and whose aim is to lead him into all truth as it is needed in his daily walk.

My prayer is that we may be taught by Him as we study together.

CHAPTER 2

THE MIND

THE first Greek word which we will examine is the word *nous* (νοῦς). Bullinger writes of this word: "The organ of mental perception and apprehension, the organ of conscious life, the organ of the consciousness preceding the act, or recognizing and judging the fact. It is *generally* the organ of thinking and knowledge, i.e., contemplation. In the New Testament (except for Luke 24:45 and Revelation 13:18 and 17:9) it occurs only in Paul's epistles, and is used of the reflective consciousness *as distinct from the impulse of the spirit apart from such consciousness.* It takes cognizance of external objects and denotes the reasoning faculty. Its chief material organ is the brain, but all the senses serve it actively or passively."

We will follow this word through the Epistle to the Romans. It is first used in Romans 1:28 where the apostle is describing the moral state of heathendom. The verse reads: "And even as they did not like to retain God in their knowledge [the Greek word implies 'a knowledge that has a powerful influence on the knower'*], God gave them over to a reprobate *mind*, to do those things which are not convenient." In other words, their deliberate attitude of the non-admission of God into their lives—they were ungodly—resulted in the prostitution of the "nous" to all kinds of moral debasement. How easy it is to mark the outworking of this law in the history of our world! How inevitably forgetfulness of God brings ruin in its train! It has been pointed out again and again, and cannot be too strongly underlined, that in our modern age intellectual attainment has so far outstripped moral progress that the creations of man's inventive genius threaten to bring our world down to utter destruction about our ears. The fear of this haunts many minds, and dictates the present course of international politics.

It next appears in two verses in Romans 7—verses 23 and 25—and it will be best to quote these verses and verse 24 in full, making any necessary comment afterwards. "But I see another law in my members, warring against the law of my *mind*, and bringing me into captivity to the law of sin which is in my members. O wretched man that I am! who shall deliver

---

* See Chapter 7.

me from the body of this death? I thank God through Jesus Christ our Lord. So then with the *mind* I myself serve the law of God; but with the flesh the law of sin." The issue is now brought down to the level of the individual as every issue must be in the end. Here is a man consciously awake to the "rightness" of the law and dealings of God. But he is immediately faced with a problem, which confronts every honest seeker after God at this stage: he finds that, although all is clear to his mind, and he knows without any outer voice telling him that he cannot go on living under the dominion of sin and at the same time serve a holy God, the law of sin working through his fallen nature pulls inexorably in the opposite direction. This man needs help, and needs it desperately! How important it is that at this juncture he may be pointed to Christ in whom alone is deliverance and not to his own unavailing struggles, until he can join in Paul's shout of praise—"I thank God—through Jesus Christ our Lord!"

Romans 11:34 speaks of "the mind of the Lord," and is not important for our study except that it applies the same word for "reflective consciousness" to both God and man, showing that this reasoning faculty is a part of God's own nature imparted to the creature.

16 / The Bible and the Human Mind

Romans 12:2 is most illuminating: "And be not conformed to this world: but ye be transformed [literally 'transfigured'] by the renewing of your *mind*, that ye may prove what is that good, and acceptable, and perfect, will of God." The secret of true Christian living is revealed here. Our "reflective consciousness" which, because of the fall has been brought into line with the thinking "of this world" of which Satan is the prince, can and must be renewed by the Holy Spirit. In this way only can we learn to think God's thoughts, to know His will, and to be incorporated into His new creation in Christ. We shall then catch and manifest some of the grace and beauty of God, a thing impossible in any other way. Reformation is not all that the gospel enjoins. Men must repent and turn to God not just to become "good citizens" or "loyal church members"—an unconverted man can be all this! Our whole mental makeup needs to be refashioned so that we may fit into God's ways, and His will may be done in our lives.

The last reference in this epistle is Romans 14:5, where we see the renewed mind in action. Paul tells us that in all doubtful questions, we are to reach our own conclusions, and maintain them lovingly, without descending to the self-opinionated dogmatism which mars so much

Christian work and witness. "Let every man be fully persuaded in his own *mind*" is his advice. We should beware of secondhand opinions, and a follow-my-leader attitude. It is our responsibility to think things out for ourselves under the deliberately sought guidance of God the Holy Spirit until we arrive at a solution that brings us assurance and peace; but it is no part of our business to seek to force others into the mold of our thinking.

Now for the other Pauline epistles. The first letter to the Corinthians has three passages in which our word appears. In 1:10 it is used in connection with Christian unity: "Now I beseech you, brethren, by the name of our Lord Jesus Christ, that ye all speak the same thing, and that there be no divisions among you; but that ye be perfectly joined together in the same *mind* and in the same judgment."* Divisions come from the old carnal nature, and discord is sown by Satan. Our objective—and our mind has no real doubt on this point—should be to be at one with our fellow believers.

1 Corinthians 2:16 also makes this clear. The latter part of this chapter insists that the work of revealing divine truth is the prerogative of God the Holy Spirit, and then closes with this verse:

---
* See Chapter 12.

"For who hath known the mind of the Lord, that he may instruct Him? *But we have the mind of Christ.*" Being a partaker of the divine nature, each believer has imparted to him the "reflective consciousness" of the Son of God as he seeks to become adjusted to it. This is an experience which humbles and unites, but never puffs up and divides. We must always bear in mind also that owing to our human limitations no Christian experience ever even approximates to perfection in this life, and that to imagine that such a verse warrants our claiming infallibility in the interpretation of Scripture is utter folly and presumption.

Lastly, 1 Corinthians 14:14–15 and 19 show very clearly Paul's view of any tendency towards passivity of mind in dealing with spiritual gifts: "For if I pray in an unknown tongue, my spirit prayeth, but my *understanding* is unfruitful. What is it then? I will pray with the spirit, and I will pray with the *understanding* also; I will sing with the spirit, and I will sing with the *understanding* also. . . . Yet in the church I had rather speak five words with my *understanding*, that by my voice I might teach others also, than ten thousand words in an unknown tongue." There should be nothing mechanical in either our approach to truth or our reception of the grace of God.

In this regard, Mrs. Jessie Penn-Lewis wrote:

> God requires one's cooperation with His Spirit, *and the full use of every faculty of the whole man.* In short, the powers of darkness aim at obtaining a passive slave, a captive to their will; while God desires a regenerated man who is intelligently and actively both willing and choosing, doing His will in liberation from slavery of spirit, soul and body.
>
> The powers of darkness would make a man a machine, a tool, an automaton; the God of holiness and love desires to make him a free, intelligent sovereign in his own sphere—a thinking, rational, renewed creation, created after His own image (Ephesians 4:24). Therefore, God never says to any faculty of man "Be thou idle"*

I have developed this at some length because most spurious religious experience which presents itself to the seeker after truth, whether a Christian or otherwise, gains its ascendancy through mental passivity. Healthy Christian living is always rational, the mind playing a positive, active role.

Two references in Ephesians 4 seem to

War on the Saints, page 75. Published by the Christian Literature Crusade.

fall naturally into place just here. In verse 17 we find the exhortation: "This I say therefore, and testify in the Lord, that ye henceforth walk not as other Gentiles walk, in the vanity of their mind"; and then verse 23 shows us the way in which this exhortation can be carried into practical effect: "And be renewed in the spirit of your *mind*." There is an infinite distance between the abysmal ignorance of the mental outlook of the unconverted man concerning God and His ways, and the enlightened thinking of the man who, through Christ, has become rightly adjusted to his Maker. A man may be an intellectual giant, and yet be completely in the dark as far as the things of God are concerned. The humblest, most uneducated believer is wiser than he. The renewing spoken of here is the work of God the Holy Spirit in the mind of the man who has been reconciled to God through the sacrifice of Calvary.

Colossians 2:18 sounds a note of warning: "Let no man beguile you of your reward in a voluntary humility and worshipping of angels, intruding into those things which he hath not seen, vainly puffed up by his fleshly *mind*, and not holding the Head. . . ." How easy it is to give way to restless and even morbid curiosity! In a day when profitless speculation about spiritual things, often divorced from practical Christian living, is rife, we shall do well to remember that all truth is found in the person of Christ, and in Him alone. "The anointing" (1 John 2:27) given to the believer is to teach him to abide in Christ, not that he may unravel spiritual puzzles. "The secret things belong unto the LORD our God: but those things which are revealed belong unto us and to our children for ever, that we may do all the words of this law" (Deuteronomy 29:29) is a basic spiritual principle, which operates in the Christian age just as it did in the life of the people of Israel.

2 Thessalonians 2:2 also urges watchfulness in this direction, and calls for great spiritual steadiness towards the various conflicting ideas of doctrine and prophecy with which we inevitably meet. Paul urges his converts not to be soon "*shaken in mind.*" This is a very real danger, especially (to keep closely to the context) in the case of the Second Coming of our Lord and Saviour, Jesus Christ. Disappointment caused, for example, by a hasty acceptance of the findings of "datefixers" may well shake a man's whole spiritual life to its foundations. Avoid these things as you would the plague, and stick close to Christ and the enjoyment of His love and constant fellowship.

22 / *The Bible and the Human Mind*

Such possible pitfalls lead on naturally to the consideration of the state of mind of those who have actually been deluded into holding and teaching some form of error. In 1 Timothy 6:3-5 Paul counsels Timothy as follows: "If any man . . . consent not to wholesome words, even the words of our Lord Jesus Christ, and to the doctrine which is according to godliness; he is proud, knowing nothing, but doting about questions and strifes of words, whereof cometh envy, strife, railings, evil surmisings, perverse disputings of men of corrupt *minds,* and destitute of the truth, supposing that gain is godliness: from such withdraw thyself." Once more the standard is set—"the doctrine which is according to godliness" or godlikeness. Man has fallen to a place far, very far, from God; but in the person of his Substitute, who bore his sin and now lives forever, he has been brought very near to God—so near that he is to be remade in His image. Anything other than this, however right and religious it may seem, comes from corruption of mind and drags men down into darkness.

2 Timothy 3:8 seems to finish this story. Speaking of those who have "a form of godliness" but who "deny the power thereof," Paul describes them as "ever learning, and never able to come to the

The Mind / 23

knowledge of the truth"; and ends: "Now as Jannes and Jambres withstood Moses, so do these also resist the truth: men of corrupt *minds*, reprobate concerning the faith. But they shall proceed no further: for their folly shall be manifest unto all men, as theirs also was." We do not need to sigh over the dark times in which we live, and deplore the spread of false cults. First we must keep ourselves clear of those things which corrupt the mind; curiosity can lead us into real danger here! Next we may trust according to the promise that our passage gives us, and ask God to give us minds so in harmony with Him that we may soon witness the folly of these things being made obvious to all.

The final reference for "nous" in Paul's letters is found in Titus 1:15, which enunciates a great spiritual principle: "Unto the pure, all things are pure: but unto them that are defiled and unbelieving is nothing pure; but even their *mind* and conscience is defiled." The one thing that matters is to be so adjusted to our Saviour that the full efficacy of His precious cleansing blood may be ours. In this way only can a man be pure and see all things with His purity of outlook. "But if we walk in the light, as He is in the light, we have fellowship one with another, and the blood of Jesus Christ His Son cleanseth us from all sin" (1 John 1:7). Outside this path lies only a fatal defilement of our understanding.

It now only remains to touch upon Luke 24:45 and the two verses in Revelation. The verse in Luke's Gospel is very striking. During His earthly ministry the disciples never really understood their Lord. This is only too plainly shown by their constant questioning and obvious bewilderment. Their minds were unable to grasp that He had come not to set up an immediate kingdom but rather to put away sin by the sacrifice of Himself. It was only after He had risen from the dead that we read: "Then opened He their *understanding, that they might understand the Scriptures.*" It was necessary that He Himself should enlighten minds darkened by the Fall—should open the meaning of Scripture to men in whom was operating the law to which Paul refers in 1 Corinthians 2:14: "But the natural man receiveth not the things of the Spirit of God: for they are foolishness unto Him: neither can He know them, because they are spiritually discerned." We are told, for instance, in John 20:9, of the disciples on the first Easter morning, that their surprise and confusion came from the fact that "they knew not the scripture, that He must rise again from the dead." And yet

He had told them again and again! Their minds had been unable to grasp what He had meant; they could not understand the significance of His rising again until they were divinely enlightened. And today also there is a great gulf between the acceptance in general terms of the great dogmas of the Christian faith and a personal knowledge of them—a true perception because God Himself has quickened our minds. In this one verse we have summed up all that is taught from various angles in the Pauline Epistles.

Finally, the two references in Revelation—Revelation 13:18 and 17:9. Here are two passages where our word is coupled with the Greek word "sophia," or "practical wisdom" (see Chapter 9). The mysteries referred to are obviously not those about which to theorize; but a time will come when men will see clearly, and shape their behavior accordingly. It is unwise to dogmatize about anything which may at the present time be only debatable and, to some extent, of academic interest. But in due time, the minds of those who need this insight will be enlightened so that they may understand. Always, our minds are quickened in order that we may know how to *live.*

*   *   *   *   *

"Conscious delight in the law of God is the peculiar characteristic of those who are born of God; it is the result of their participation in the enjoyment of the blessings of the new covenant: 'I will put My laws into their mind, and write them in their hearts . . . for I will be merciful to their unrighteousness, and their sins and their iniquities will I remember no more' (Hebrews 8:10–12). How otherwise *could* a man delight in the law whose existence condemned him?

"The original word 'delight' is not elsewhere used in the New Testament; it is derived from a word which signifies pleasure or sweetness, and here refers to that which is supremely attractive, pleasant, and delightful to the soul. . . .

"Now, as the law of grace reaches unto every part of a regenerate man, so is there in him a something of evil for grace to deal with in every faculty of his soul; and, in fact, there are as many laws of sin in the corrupt human heart as there are revealed laws of God in Scripture. The author of this seventh chapter of the Epistle to the Romans had found out the mystery of iniquity within him. 'I see a law in my members warring against the law of my mind.' By this law of his mind he means the law of the Lord written in his heart, as we have seen."

The Mind / 27

(Rev. Marcus Rainsford on Romans 7:22–23)

*   *   *   *   *

"Here we may learn: (1) That *facts* or truths will yet remove the *mysteries* that we now see in religion. (2) That our prejudices and our preconceived opinions are one cause of our seeing so many mysteries in the Bible. If a man is willing to take the plain declarations of the Bible, he will be little perplexed with mysteries. (3) God alone can overcome our prejudices—open our hearts—and dispose us to receive the engrafted word with meekness, and with the simplicity of a child. (See Acts 16:14; James 1:21; Mark 10:15.) (4) The design of God's opening the understanding is that we may be acquainted with the Scriptures. It is not that we may be made wise above what is written, but that we may submit ourselves wholly to the Word of God."

(Rev. Albert Barnes on Luke 24:45)

CHAPTER 3

THOUGHTS

ANOTHER Greek word, one which is important in examining the teaching of Scripture concerning the mind, is the word *noēma* (νόημα). Bullinger says of it: "The product of the action of the '*nous*,' that which is thought out, excogitated; purpose, project, device, the thoughts." This does not need further elaboration except to say that we are now dealing with the thinking, reasoning part of man finding expression in *thoughts, ideas* or *projects.*

The word is used four times in the Second Epistle to the Corinthians, once in the Epistle to the Philippians, and once with the preposition *dia* prefixed in Luke 11:17.

The Corinthian passages contain a wealth of information, and we will take them in the order in which they occur. In 2 Corinthians 3:14 we find that Paul, in speaking of the people of Israel, reminds his readers that when Moses came down from Mount Sinai, where he received the Law direct from God Himself, he had to veil his face because of the reflected glory of Jehovah. Then he adds: "But their *minds* were blinded: for until this day remaineth the same veil untaken away in the reading of the Old Testament; which veil is done away in Christ. But even unto this day, when Moses is read, the veil is upon their heart. Nevertheless when it shall turn to the Lord, the veil shall be taken away." Trembling with fear, the Israelites had requested that God's communication to them not come direct from Him but rather through Moses, secondhand (Exodus 20:18–19). The result—their minds being out of touch with God, their thoughts and concepts became "blinded"; or as the American Standard Version puts it, "hardened." The Greek word here, *pōroō* (πωρόω), literally means (a) to petrify, to turn to stone; and (b) to harden, to make callous.

The preacher of the gospel is deeply conscious of the aptness of this word. What could seem more "petrified" or "callous" towards the winsomeness of the Lord Jesus than the thinking of the professedly religious man, whether Jew or Gentile, whose worship is a thing of externals ministered to him secondhand through the liturgy of his church, or perhaps the eloquence of his minister, instead of through personal contact with God, through Christ. There is only one cure for such "petrification," so that not only the thoughts but the whole man may be melted into humble trust in and love towards the living God—and that is a heart-surrender to the claims of the Lord Jesus Christ, who loves us and gave Himself for us. Until then, religion or no religion, the veil remains, and our thoughts cannot penetrate beyond or catch a glimpse of the glory of God.

In the next chapter we find our word used again: "But if our gospel be hid, it is hid to them that are lost: in whom the god of this world hath blinded the *minds* of them which believe not, lest the light of the glorious gospel of Christ, who is the image of God, should shine unto them" (4:3–4). The verb used for "blind" here is a different Greek word, *tuphoō* (τυφόω), meaning "to blind, dull, baffle." One is almost reminded of a game of blindman's buff, where one of the players, with a cloth of some kind covering his eyes, feels helplessly round a room trying to catch one of the other players, all of whom are making sport of him. It is a little startling to realize that the perceptions and theories of our most brilliant minds are baffled by

Satan, unless they have living contact with God through our Lord and Saviour Jesus Christ. But that is the fact! Is it any wonder that the international scene is chaotic in the extreme? Unbelief creates its own judgment of baffling darkness.

2 Corinthians 10:3–5 gives us our word in a rather different setting. The Apostle Paul is writing in an aggressive strain: "For though we walk in the flesh, we do not war after the flesh: (For the weapons of our warfare are not carnal, but mighty through God to the pulling down of strongholds), casting down imaginations [see Chapter 4], and every high thing that exalteth itself against the knowledge of God, and bringing into captivity every *thought* to the obedience of Christ." The preacher of the gospel is here pictured on the offensive. By dint of his proper weapons of prayer and preaching he is seeing the strongholds of sin, indifference, scepticism and unbelief thrown down; and the hearers' very thoughts are brought into captivity not to his doctrines, nor to his personality, but to Christ Himself. This is surely the object of all ministry: to bring into being a new life, which instead of being swayed this way and that by the swirling currents of theory and the thrashing problems of life is safely an-

chored in Christ. Here is true sanity and balance!

2 Corinthians 11:3 strikes a note of warning: "But I fear," writes Paul, "lest by any means, as the serpent beguiled Eve through his subtility, so your *minds* should be corrupted from the simplicity that is in Christ." In the garden of Eden the adversary conjured up before Eve alluring pictures of power and freedom, and thus deceived her; and very real danger lies just here. Is it not amazing to see how men's thoughts are colored by the same specious promises today? Most people have wrong thoughts about God, and imagine that He is in some way trying to filch from them their liberty. The truth is that there is no real freedom apart from bondslavery to Jesus Christ. Complicated theological concepts and knowledge of "advanced truth" are no signs of genuine spiritual growth. The utter simplicity of love for and communion with the Lord Jesus Christ Himself is the sum total of holy living. How particular we need to be that our "perceptions" of the character of God shall be simple, gleaned only from the Word of God. Only then shall the consequent purposes and design of life be unspoiled by the tortuous, complicated, egocentric twist so easily given to our thinking by the enemy of souls.

If this last reference sounds out a warning, our next passage, Philippians 4:6-7, brings uplift and encouragement to every believer: "Be careful for nothing," or better in the Revised Standard Version: "Have no anxiety about anything" it runs—"but in everything by prayer and supplication with thanksgiving let your requests be made known unto God. And the peace of God, which passeth all understanding, shall keep your hearts and *minds* through Christ Jesus." "Keep" is here a military word, meaning "to keep guard" or "set a garrison in." If in simple childlike trust you and I lay all our needs before our Heavenly Father, then He Himself will set the garrison of His peace in our hearts, and even in our thoughts. In this way we may be maintained in the experience of which the prophet speaks: "Thou wilt keep him in perfect peace whose mind is stayed on Thee; because he trusteth in Thee" (Isaiah 26:3).

The reference, Luke 11:17, which reads "But He, knowing their *thoughts* . . ." is of importance because it brings out the fact that every thought of man is open before the eyes of God. In this passage the Lord Jesus is facing those who, "tempting Him, sought for a sign from heaven." He saw all that was going through their minds. The Lord's knowledge of our thoughts could be a terrifying realization, but it can also be fraught with the greatest comfort to those who are His. He does not regard merely the outward action; the controlling motive, the thought behind the act, the loving desire to serve Him—all these things are open to Him, and may be a source of joy to His heart.

* * * * *

"The peace of God . . . shall keep your hearts and *minds*—literally and better, *thoughts*, acts of mind. The holy serenity of the believer's spirit in Christ Jesus shall be the immediate means of shielding even the details of mental action from the tempter's power."

(Bishop Moule on Philippians 4:7)

CHAPTER 4

THE BALANCING OF IDEAS

A TRULY interesting word is *dialogismos* (διαλογισμός), which Liddell and Scott's Lexicon renders as (a) a balancing of accounts, (b) consideration, reasoning, and (c) conversation, arguing. The root is the same as the verb sometimes rendered "reckon" in the New Testament.

It is used in Matthew 15:19 and the parallel passage Mark 7:21, linked with two adjectives translated "evil," where we are told that "out of the heart proceed evil *thoughts*. . . ." This gives us another slant on the whole question of the thought life. It is the corrupt heart of man that sifts and reasons out the ideas that are put into the mind, and finally imparts to them its own bias. The supposed advantages, for example, of sin, are weighed up, found to be to the taste, and then finally put into action in the life.

In Luke's Gospel our word is used on several occasions. The first is in Luke

2:34–35. Simeon is speaking prophetically to Mary: "Behold, this Child is set for the fall and rising again of many in Israel; and for a sign which shall be spoken against; (yea, a sword shall pierce through thy own soul also), that the *thoughts* of many hearts may be revealed." "What think ye of Christ?" is the burning question which faces all men as individuals, and their eternal destiny hangs on the answer they give from the heart—their reasoned balancing of accounts. Each man must decide for himself: can he, will he, trust himself into the keeping of the Saviour, of whom the Scriptures give so clear a picture?

In Luke 5:22 and 6:8 we are again given a glimpse (see Chapter 3) of the insight possessed by the Lord Jesus into the hearts of men. In the first instance He is dealing with the man with the palsy, and reasoning is going on in the hearts of those standing by: "Who can forgive sins but God alone?" In the second case the Lord Jesus is faced by the man with the withered hand in the synagogue on the Sabbath day, and the scribes are watching Him. "Is He going to break the Sabbath? Is He going to disregard the man's need?" They are bent on guarding their carefully observed dogmas and ceremonies at all costs; and some of them are

The Balancing of Ideas / 39

probably feeling satisfied that either way they will be able to hurl an accusation at Him. And He is conscious of it all!

In Luke 9:46–47 the Lord is dealing with His own disciples. "Then there arose a *reasoning* among them, which of them should be the greatest" (v. 46). Here is a case where heart and thought wrestle with a problem propounded first by the heart, with its natural desire for self-exaltation. Behind His back this led to a heated argument—"And Jesus, perceiving the *thought* of their heart. . . ." Again we must notice how closely heart and mind work together. There is no such thing as unbelief that is purely intellectual. We like to think that there is, but the fact is that unbelief is a result of the heart working its will upon the thoughts, and producing convincing arguments which render unbelief reasonable to its own satisfaction.

The last use of our word in this Gospel is in Luke 24:37–38. The disciples are gathered in the upper room on the first Easter Day, and suddenly Jesus is in the midst: "But they were terrified and affrighted, and supposed that they had seen a spirit. And He said unto them, Why are ye troubled? And why do *thoughts* arise in your hearts?" What to them had seemed at the time the disaster of the cross had chilled their hearts, and whenever a ray of hope from some memory of His teaching came filtering through into their minds, it was immediately reasoned out of court as being too good to be true. How often you and I are found in the same case! I can remember so well talking to a friend who was touching the depths of despair. "You cannot tell me anything!" he said. "I know all the passages of Scripture which are supposed to meet my case." It was a heartwarming vision of the love of Christ he needed, and his heart, like ours, was slow—so slow—to respond, and joyfully reckon on those things his mind knew.

In the Epistle to the Romans our word is used twice. First we find it in Romans 1:21–22, where it is again spoken of as allied to the heart: "Because that, when they knew God, they glorified Him not as God, neither were thankful; but became vain in their *imaginations* [*reasonings*—A.S.V.], and their foolish heart was darkened. Professing themselves to be wise, they became fools." The heart is once again in the ascendant, and the thoughts—contrary to reason—are made to harmonize with the heart's wish to shut God out. In dealing with others, this often gives a clue to work on. You cannot argue against a perverse heart, but must wait until the Spirit of God touches the heart

The Balancing of Ideas / 41

and it is ready to allow the thoughts to fix themselves on the Saviour.

In Romans 14:1 we are told, "Him that is weak in the faith receive ye, but not to doubtful *disputations*." Mental juggling about legal details never gets us anywhere. The man who is weak in the faith needs to be pointed to Christ and brought into touch with Him.

1 Corinthians 3:20 is quoted from Psalm 94:11: "The Lord knoweth the *thoughts* of the wise, that they are vain." Every "balancing of accounts" which leaves God out of the reckoning is utterly empty. Men—even Christian men—are often so wise in their own eyes that they feel that they can have a quiet laugh at those who always speak of God as the only final factor worth considering in any set of circumstances. The fact is, however, that he only is truly wise who never reasons without setting God in the center. We can reason, for instance, about guilt, and our hearts will tell us just how guilty we are until we despair of mercy; but place Calvary in that central place, where God has put it, and we see things in their right proportion, and find that guilt is dealt with by grace, and sin put away by mercy.

"Do all things," writes Paul again, "without murmurings and *disputings*" (Philippians 2:14). He has been pointing to the necessity for each Christian to walk in humble obedience, working out the salvation that has been put into him in Christ, because "it is God that worketh in you both to will and to do of His good pleasure." Reasoning against and arguing with God is therefore going to be the one real bar to godly living. He must control the heart, which will otherwise impose once more its evil sway upon both mind and thoughts.

In 1 Timothy 2:8 our word is used in much the same setting, this time with special reference to prayer: "I will therefore that men pray everywhere, lifting up holy hands, without wrath and *doubting*." In prayer we are not dealing with those things which would appear reasonable to men, we are looking into the realm where God is; and heart and mind are satisfied when they reckon on Him alone. "The fact that our Almighty Father," wrote George Muller of Bristol, "who is full of infinite love to us His children, and who has proved to us His love in the gift of His only Begotten Son, and shown His almighty power in raising Him from the dead, knows that we have need of these things, should remove all anxiety from our minds." There is no room here for those reasonings which cast doubt either on

The Balancing of Ideas / 43

God's willingness or ability to hear and answer prayer.

The final use of this word is in James 2:4 where the apostle is remonstrating with his readers about the wrong of showing favoritism to the rich. "Are ye not then partial in yourselves?" he then asks, "and are become judges of evil *thoughts*?" Again the heart makes its distinctions and leaves it to the mind to provide its reasons for so doing—a fact of which we must never lose sight.

The word *logismos* (λογισμός)—the same word without the strengthening preposition *dia*, is used twice in the New Testament. In Romans 2:15 Paul writes of those who "shew the work of the law written in their hearts, their conscience also bearing witness, and their *thoughts* the meanwhile accusing or else excusing one another." Again we find the aliance of heart and mind, weighing up right and wrong, balancing one against the other, and either accepting the accusation as a true bill or building up a system of excuse.

In 2 Corinthians 10:3–5 it is translated "*imaginations,*" and appears in a passage which has already been mentioned (see Chapter 3), where Paul is discussing the warfare of Christian ministry. In the American Standard Version it reads, "For though we walk in the flesh, we do not war according to the flesh (for the weapons of our warfare are not of the flesh, but mighty before God to the casting down of strongholds); casting down *imaginations,* and every high thing that is exalted against the knowledge of God, and bringing every thought into captivity to the obedience of Christ." The mighty operation of the Spirit of God through the truth of God is able to break through the alliance of heart and mind which builds up such strongholds of doubt and argument, until even the thoughts are brought to "the obedience of Christ." This is the work of the Christian ministry in relation to the thoughts of men.

CHAPTER 5

THE INTELLECT

ANOTHER Greek word translated "mind" in Scripture, which it will be necessary to examine in some detail, is *dianoia*, (διανοίᾳ) which Liddell & Scott's Lexicon tells us means (a) a thought, intention, purpose; (b) the faculty of thought, intellect (opp. to body), generally—mind; (c) a notion or belief.

According to Bullinger it is used twelve times in the New Testament, one of which is a doubtful rendering.

In Matthew 22:37, Mark 12:30 and Luke 10:27 the divine summary of the Law is given to us in familiar words: "Thou shalt love the Lord thy God with all thy heart, and with all thy soul, and with all thy *mind*; and thy neighbour as thyself." Mark and Luke add the word "strength" as well, bringing the whole man into the picture. The love for which God asks is not only that of the heart and emotions, but it is an informed, intelligent love based on knowledge of Him and His ways. It would seem even to embrace the strength and vigor of the physical frame devoted to His service. This is a vital principle of all spiritual life. God does not ask us to trust Him blindly, as so many imagine. He has given us faculties of intelligence which are quickened by the gift of eternal life, which is the knowledge of Him (see John 17:3). We may discern Him through His Word, watch Him at work in the circumstances of life, and learn the grace and kindness of His dealings under the tutelage of God the Holy Spirit.

Four significant passages in Paul's epistles deal with the "dianoia" of the unconverted man. The first is Ephesians 2:1-3: "And you hath he quickened, who were dead in trespasses and sins; wherein in times past ye walked according to the course of this world, according to the prince of the power of the air, the spirit that now worketh in the children of disobedience: among whom also we all had our conversation in times past in the lusts of our flesh, fulfilling the desires of the flesh and of the *mind*; and were by nature the children of wrath, even as others." In these verses we have depicted the world of men under the rule of Satan, dominated either by the desires of the flesh—the lower, sensual realm of human nature; or the mind—the higher, cultured, thinking side of man's makeup. The gross sins of the flesh are by no means the only, or even perhaps the most dangerous, errors to which man is subject. The self-centered intellectual conceptions of men whose thinking is not subordinated to God have been responsible for the bulk of the wrongs and sufferings of the human race. History bears evidence to this fact. What chains man has fastened on his fellows by the brilliance of his native wit in planning his own aggrandizement! Our world today reveals the inextricable muddle of which our fallen intellect is capable.

We find this line of teaching amplified in Ephesians 4:18, where unconverted men are described as "having the *understanding* darkened, being alienated from the life of God through the ignorance that is in them, because of the blindness of their heart"; and again in Colossians 1:21 Paul addresses Christians as "You that were sometime alienated and enemies in your *mind* by wicked works." Psychology explores the manifold ramifications of the human mind, but failing to grasp the true state of man's thought life in its relationship to God, it relinquishes the one key capable of bringing his inner being to real health, sanity and balance.

Ephesians 1:17-18 is our one debatable passage, where most authorities substitute the Greek word "kardia," meaning "heart," for our word "dianoia." Nevertheless this verse shows the one way of right thinking. Paul is praying for the Christians of Ephesus "that the God of our Lord Jesus Christ, the Father of glory, may give unto you the spirit of wisdom and revelation in the knowledge of Him: the eyes of your *understanding* being enlightened; that ye might know . . ." for Christian experience is based not on ideas but upon revealed knowledge—a solid foundation indeed!

John confirms this fact. "And we know," he writes, "that the Son of God is come, and hath given us an *understanding*, that we may know Him that is true, and we are in Him that is true, even in His Son Jesus Christ. This is the true God, and eternal life. Little children, keep yourselves from idols. Amen" (1 John 5:20-21). He is not afraid to assert dogmatically the possibility of knowing God for oneself, and of placing all other conceptions of religion in the category of idolatry. He is right! It is indeed possible to set up as idols the ideas and conceptions of our minds, instead of fashioning statues with our hands, and falling down before them; and in the end

The Intellect / 49

it may prove just as dangerous and degrading.

The writer to the Hebrews twice speaks of God's purpose to enlighten the darkness of the human intellect in those who enter into His new covenant of grace given to mankind in Jesus Christ. "I will put My laws into their mind, and write them in their hearts: and I will be to them a God, and they shall be to me a people: and they shall not teach every man his neighbour, and every man his brother, saying, Know the Lord: for all shall know Me, from the least to the greatest" (Hebrews 8:10–11). The knowledge of God is not the prerogative of a privileged class of religious middlemen, but belongs to all alike "from the least to the greatest." Hebrews 10:16 repeats the same thought, and also uses our word "dianoia."

The two final references occur in Peter's epistles. The first is an exhortation given in light of the magnificence of our Christian heritage, and the opposition and testing to be faced by believers in a fallen environment—"Wherefore," he urges, "gird up the loins of your *mind*, be sober, and hope to the end for the grace that is to be brought unto you at the revelation of Jesus Christ" (1 Peter 1:13). There can be no mental passivity in the pursuit of truth. God has made us reasoning, thinking beings and deals with us as such. The mind must be disciplined and exercised, and not permitted to drift with every crosscurrent of thought submitted to it. A blank, flabby mind is a grave disorder and leads into danger.

In his Second Epistle he writes: "This second epistle, beloved, I now write unto you; in both which I stir up your pure *minds* by way of remembrance" (2 Peter 3:1). The Greek word for pure used here literally translated means "examined by the sun's light," and therefore "pure." It is through divinely created light that our intellectual capacity can be brought into harmony with God. Paul puts it this way: "For God, who commanded the light to shine out of darkness, hath shined in our hearts, to give the light of the knowledge of the glory of God in the face of Jesus Christ" (2 Corinthians 4:6). Here is the one source of Christian life and experience, and the objective of Christian ministry—"In Thy light shall we see light" (Psalm 36:9).

Perhaps it will not be out of place to add here a word which only occurs once in the New Testament—*epinoia* (ἐπίνοια). The dictionary translates it as "cogitation, purpose, device." It is used in Acts 8:22: Simon the magician has offered the apostles money if they will impart to him

The Intellect / 51

the gift of conferring on others the indwelling of the Holy Spirit. His thinking is all wrong. He views divine gifts as a mere occasion for satisfying his own desire for prominence, and as having a cash value. "Repent therefore of this thy wickedness," Peter exhorts him, "and pray God, if perhaps the *thought* of thine heart may be forgiven thee." How man's thinking has to be revolutionized if he is to have fellowship with God; and the change must begin in the heart.

* * * * *

"Surrender your God-endowed powers to be passively moulded by authority—any form of authority standing between you and the book of Nature or Revelation either—consent to think by proxy on any subject civil or religious, and your history may soon be told. Mental stagnation and non-growth will be your inheritance while you remain on the earth, and a long oblivion will cover your memory when you leave it."

(Rev. Asa Mahan, an Exeter Hall Lecturer, 1849/50)

* * * * *

"In Ephesians 1:18 we read: 'The eyes of your understanding being enlightened.' Here is the mind illumined by the Spirit.

It is the vehicle of light. You *see* with the mind, you *feel* with the spirit. David said, 'My *spirit* made diligent search.' The mind is filled with light from God in the spirit, illuminating the mind. This brings into action the perceptive faculty of the mind, whereby the believer is able to spiritually discern spiritual things. The various marginal readings of 1 Corinthians 2:13 show the new mind in use. It is able to 'discriminate,' 'examine,' 'combine,' 'compare,' and 'explain' spiritual things which the 'natural' man knows nothing about. The perceptive faculty of the mind renewed by the Spirit of God enables us more clearly to know how to prove the good and acceptable will of God."

(Mrs. Penn-Lewis in *The Battle for the Mind*)

CHAPTER 6

UNDERSTANDING

AN important group of words is that which has a common root in the verb *ginōskō* (γινώσκω). The most commonly used of these is the word *gnōsis* (γνῶσις). This is used twenty-nine times in the New Testament, and the meaning given by the Lexicons can be summarized as follows: "knowing, or recognition—the *knowledge* or *understanding* of a thing; the insight which manifests itself through understanding of subjects with which it meets, and in conduct determined thereby." There is no passivity in such a word. The mind is pictured actively laying hold of those things brought to its ken, and vigorously determining its response to them.

In the Gospels it appears twice only, and is used on both occasions by Luke. It is employed in a verse very familiar to those who are accustomed to the Church of England service—Luke 1:77: "To give *knowledge* of salvation unto His people by the remission of their sins. . . ." A clear grasp of the plan of salvation made possible by the sacrifice of Calvary is the essential foundation upon which alone the knowledge of God can be built. The second occasion of its use in this Gospel is in strong contrast to the first. It is found in Luke 11:52, when the charges leveled by the Lord Jesus against the scribes reach their climax: "Woe unto you, lawyers! for ye have taken away the key of *knowledge*: ye entered not in yourselves, and them that were entering in ye hindered." They had so cluttered up the minds of the people with petty distinctions and trivial legal points of doctrine and ritual that they had effectually hidden the one key to the gateway into life—the slain Lamb. What an indictment! And what a responsibility that man incurs today who hides the full glory of the gospel under a mass of empty words and trite phrases, and thus makes void the cross of Christ!

The epistles of Paul contain the bulk of the remainder of the places where our word is used. Romans has three. In Romans 2:20 the Jews are told that in the Law they possess the "embodiment of *knowledge*" (R.S.V.); in Romans 11:33 a cry of wonder is wrung from the apostle as he considers the greatness and splendor of God's *knowledge*; and in Romans

15:14 Paul tells the Romans that he is persuaded that they are "filled with all *knowledge*," and therefore able (and this is a point to be noted in these days when so many are dependent upon so few for spiritual light) to "admonish one another."

In the First Epistle to the Corinthians our word is used on a number of occasions, and we find that some of the dangers with which the Christian path is surrounded are unmasked. In 1 Corinthians 1:5 Paul bears witness that here is a church "in everything . . . enriched by Him, in all utterance, and in all *knowledge*"; and yet shortly after he charges them with carnality because of their divisions; and worse, with unchecked, undealt-with sin. In other words, this church had this in common with the world about it: its knowledge had outrun its morals. Knowledge, even knowledge of spiritual things, does not necessarily bring a man into fellowship with God; it must run in double harness with obedience to His Word and will.

Chapter 8 is particularly interesting, and uses this word no less than five times. We can possibly summarize the teaching of these passages as follows: There was no doubt at all of the insight possessed by these Corinthian Christians of the rights and wrongs of such subjects as "things offered unto idols," but such knowledge, we are warned, is liable to "puff up" and give a sense of superiority. All our knowledge is strictly limited and often warped by our finite minds, and we must therefore be careful not to boast of our knowledge about doctrines and practical teachings; nor must we exalt knowledge out of its rightful proportions. The genuine knowledge of God is born of love (verses 1–3). It is not given to all to have knowledge easily of those things which either need to be done or to be avoided (verse 7). We must, therefore, if we are well instructed ourselves, recognize that a trust is committed to us, and our knowledge is at all costs to be used in such a way that others may be helped and not stumbled. This is our solemn responsibility (verses 10–11).

Finally, as far as this epistle is concerned, we come to four references in chapters 12, 13 and 14, the special subject of which is "spiritual gifts." The first reference in 1 Corinthians 12:8 speaks of "the word of *knowledge*" as one of the gifts allotted to believers by the Holy Spirit according to His will. In chapter 13 all gifts are seen in their proper perspective in relationship to the great central fact and necessity of the Christian life—love. In verse 2 we are told: "Though I have . . .

all *knowledge,* . . . and have not charity, I am nothing." Then in verses 8–10: "Charity never faileth . . . whether there be *knowledge,* it shall vanish away. For we know in part, and we prophesy in part. But when that which is perfect is come, then that which is in part shall be done away." I am sure of one thing—that a true understanding of spiritual values teaches us above all how truly limited our knowledge is, and that it therefore breeds in us a deep, enduring humility, which is possibly the greatest of all graces. Then in 14:6 our word is used to correct a disposition among some, not unknown in our day, to exaggerate the value of speaking in tongues: "Now, brethren, if I come unto you speaking with tongues, what shall I profit you, except I shall speak to you either by revelation, or by *knowledge*, or by prophesying, or by doctrine?" We must always bear in mind that spiritual gifts are never imparted to us for our own benefit or enjoyment, but in order that they may be employed under the driving force of love for the profit and blessings of others.

The Second Epistle to the Corinthians provides us with six more references. The first is 2 Corinthians 2:14—"Now thanks be unto God, which always causeth us to triumph in Christ, and maketh manifest the savour of his *knowledge* by us in every place." Here is outlined the logical outworking of the triumph of Christ in the life of the individual—that the knowledge of Him, not just the truth about Him, may be spread through all the world. Such knowledge can only be manifested by those who are gripped and held fast by it. Then in 2 Corinthians 4:6 Paul writes: "For God, who commanded the light to shine out of darkness, hath shined in our hearts, to give the light of the *knowledge* of the glory of God in the face of Jesus Christ." This is a radiant knowledge which finds initial lodgment not in the head but in the heart. It is a transfiguring knowledge, in the light of which all things are made new.

Our next reference, 2 Corinthians 6:6, shows knowledge to be one of the necessary equipments of the Christian worker, and it is worth noting the other qualities which appear side by side with it: "By pureness, by *knowledge*, by longsuffering, by kindness, by the Holy Ghost, by love unfeigned." None of these can be brought about by a mere academic knowledge of Christian truth, but they speak of a deep work of God in the heart.

Next we find, as is perhaps fitting, a place in which Paul uses our word in his exhortation to the members of this church to liberality—2 Corinthians 8:7: "Therefore, as ye abound in everything, in faith, and utterance, and *knowledge*, and in all diligence, and in your love to us, see that ye abound in this grace also."

In 10:3–5 we come again to a passage we have quoted twice already (see Chapters 3 and 4) where Paul extols the spiritual equipment of the minister of Jesus Christ as being well able to cast down "every high thing that exalteth itself against the *knowledge* of God. . . ."

In 2 Corinthians 11:6 our word appears for the last time in this epistle. Paul is embarked on an impassioned plea that his warnings and teachings shall be heeded. "But though I be rude in speech," he writes, "yet not in *knowledge*." He may not, he says in effect, have always expressed himself in a way that would commend itself to the artistic taste of Corinth, but they cannot deny that he is speaking from firsthand personal knowledge. May you and I be able to make a similar claim! It is of little value if we preach eloquently and fascinate the minds of our hearers, if behind our words the genuine power of personal knowledge is lacking.

In Ephesians 3:19 we have one of Paul's lovely, and at a casual glance seemingly extravagant, outbursts. He speaks of "the love of Christ, which passeth *knowledge*," and how true it is that the length, and depth, and breadth, and height of His love will always be beyond our understanding until by infinite grace we "know as we are known."

The letters to Philippi and Colosse each contain one reference. In Philippians 3:8 is Paul's proud boast—"Yea doubtless, and I count all things but loss for the excellency of the *knowledge* of Christ Jesus my Lord. . . ." What, after all, can compare with the knowledge of Him! We cannot afford to be slipshod in our thinking here. Sit down deliberately and weigh it up! Is there anything in all the world we can possibly throw into the scales which can outweigh it? Of course not! Then shall we not pursue it with all our might? In Colossians 2:2–3 Paul points to the source and spring of all true knowledge—"Christ, in whom are hid all the treasures of wisdom, and *knowledge.*" God has through the workings of nature hidden seams of coal in the earth for the benefit of man, which man must find and bring to the surface and put into use. So He has hidden in Christ all the riches of true wisdom, a prize to the man who will turn away from all else and dig deep for himself, and bring out this wealth for his own use and the benefit of all around him.

Peter uses our word four times. First in

1 Peter 3:7: "Likewise, ye husbands, dwell with them according to *knowledge,* giving honour unto the wife, as unto the weaker vessel, and as being heirs together of the grace of life, that your prayers be not hindered." Where Christ is known and loved there will be no need for the help of a marriage guidance counselor, but a sweet, balanced home life will result.

In the first chapter of Peter's second letter he uses it in the list of those facets of Christian character that need to be added to faith, and it is worth noting carefully the qualities with which it is linked. "Add to virtue ["moral excellencies" is the literal translation of this word] *knowledge*, and to knowledge temperance [self-control] . . ." (2 Peter 1:5–6). It is obviously calamitous ever to divorce what God has joined, and we shall do well to see that our knowledge is always kept in the closest association with these balancing traits of Christian personality.

Our final reference is 2 Peter 3:17–18, which seems a suitable close to this section of our study. Peter ends his letter with these words, which call for no comment: "Ye therefore, beloved, seeing ye know these things before, beware lest ye also, being led away with the error of the wicked, fall from your own steadfastness. But grow in grace, and in the *knowledge* of our Lord and Saviour Jesus Christ. To Him be glory both now and for ever. Amen."

*   *   *   *   *

"What the Holy Ghost reveals and imparts is the knowledge of realities which are eternal in God. He brings a *living* knowledge; His light is the light of life. It is not information, an insight into the connection of truths and an appreciation of their beauty and grandeur. Men may have such knowledge vast and deep and yet be destitute of the grace of God and uninhabited by the divine Spirit."

(Dr. A. Saphir, *Christ Crucified*)

CHAPTER 7

FULL UNDERSTANDING

IN the previous chapter "gnosis" was the word under examination, and in this chapter we propose to study another word having the same root—*epignōsis* (ἐπίγνωσις). This is a stronger word and expresses "a more thorough participation on the part of the knower with the object of knowledge; a knowledge that has a powerful influence on the knower."

It is used on twenty occasions in the New Testament, sixteen of which are to be found in the Pauline Epistles. In the first place we will examine three interesting occurrences in the letter to the Romans. The pagan nations, we are told in Romans 1:28 (see Chapters 1 and 4), "did not like to retain God in their *knowledge*"; they resisted the influence that such a knowledge was bound to have on their lives, and therefore "God gave them over to a reprobate mind, to do those things which are not convenient." It is not possible to play fast and loose with divine revelation, even that given through nature, without reaping a harvest of mental twists that, in their wake, bring moral corruption.

Next our word is used to give us a correct slant on the place occupied by the Law of Moses in the Christian life—Romans 3:20: "Therefore by the deeds of the law there shall no flesh be justified in His sight: for by the law is the *knowledge* of sin." The Law, by its very impossibility of fulfillment by fallen man, serves both to depict sin and show us our powerlessness to grapple with it, and to convince us that Christ alone can save. Here is the real function of the Law.

Then in Romans 10:1-4 Paul sums up the need of, and his longing for, his own folk in these words: "Brethren, my heart's desire and prayer to God for Israel is, that they might be saved. For I bear them record that they have a zeal of God, but not according to *knowledge*." Then he explains precisely what he means by this last phrase—"For they being ignorant of God's righteousness, and going about to establish their own righteousness, have not submitted themselves unto the righteousness of God." Zeal without knowledge is still a common trap for the unwary; and it is only too easy, even with an evangelical background, to live a life of

Full Understanding / 65

religious energy but to depend upon our own efforts rather than the gracious provision of a full salvation in Christ.

In the letter to the Ephesians our word is used twice; on the first occasion—Ephesians 1:17—in the prayer offered by the apostle for the members of this church: "That the God of our Lord Jesus Christ, the Father of glory, may give unto you the spirit of wisdom and revelation in the *knowledge* of Him" (see Chapter 4). We must note the emphasis, which has come to the fore again and again in our studies—knowledge not of things, ideas, or doctrines, but of a Person. Here is a knowledge having a powerful influence on the knower. It is the knowledge of a Father who loves, of a Saviour who died for us and lives again, and of the Holy Spirit as One who, by His controlling power, is able to help in every circumstance of life.

The other verse in this letter is Ephesians 4:13, which places before us the ultimate goal of all Christian work and ministry: "Till we all come in the unity of the faith, and of the *knowledge* of the Son of God, unto a perfect man, unto the measure of the stature of the fulness of Christ." Trusting in Him, we come to know Him ever more perfectly for ourselves; and as we are drawn closer to Him in fellowship with our fellow members of the Body of Christ, we become like Him until the great consummation of conformity to His image is at last reached.

In Philippians 1:9 Paul is again praying: "And this I pray, that your love may abound yet more and more in *knowledge* and in all judgment [perception]." Note the order! First love, in which the whole life is rooted, leading to an ever increasing knowledge and the ability to discern the will of God and understand His ways.

Colossians 1:9-10 again takes us behind the scenes, and we are permitted to see something of the burden of the apostle's praying: "For this cause we also, since the day we heard it, do not cease to pray for you, and to desire that ye might be filled with the *knowledge* of His will in all wisdom and spiritual understanding; that ye might walk worthy of the Lord unto all pleasing, being fruitful in every good work, and increasing in the *knowledge* of God." The transforming knowledge of God's perfect will along with a continually developing knowledge of God Himself is something we should each set our faces towards; and also, if we are Christian workers, for those committed to our care. No lesser objective can be of lasting value.

In yet another place in this epistle, Paul uses our word as he prays—Colossians

Full Understanding / 67

2:2: "That their hearts might be comforted, being knit together in love, and unto all riches of the full assurance of understanding, to the *acknowledgement* of [that they may *know*—A.S.V.] the mystery of God, and of the Father, and of Christ." Once more we see all Paul's energies of mind and spirit bent upon one single purpose—that men might know God, and that that knowledge might revolutionize their lives.

The final appearance of this word in this letter is in Colossians 3:10, where we are shown the means by which the new man, brought into being in us by the new birth, will develop as we put off the old man by faith and put on the new—"the new man, which is renewed in *knowledge* after the image of Him that created him." There is no mystical magic in this, but enlightenment as to the nature and purposes of God, which develops and renews the new life in us day by day to that great goal which we have already glimpsed in other passages—conformity to Christ.

Our word is used four times in the Pastoral Epistles. In 1 Timothy 2:3–4: "God our Saviour, who will have all men to be saved, and to come unto the *knowledge* of the truth." In 2 Timothy 2:25–26: "In meekness instructing those that oppose themselves; if God peradventure will give them repentance to the *acknowledging* of the truth [unto the *knowledge* of the truth—A.S.V.]; and that they may recover themselves out of the snare of the devil, who are taken captive by him at his will." 2 Timothy 3:7—"Ever learning, and never able to come to the *knowledge* of the truth" (see Chapter 1). Finally in Titus 1:1: "Paul, a servant of God, and an apostle of Jesus Christ, according to the faith of God's elect, and the *acknowledging* [*knowledge*—A.S.V.] of the truth which is after godliness." These four passages will well repay thoughtful study, revealing as they do the liberating, saving power of the truth understood in that way that "has a powerful influence on the knower," offering more than a hint about the danger of pursuing mere mental knowledge without ever reaching the heart knowledge of the living God, and emphasizing the need of patient instruction of those who are outside the way of truth.

The little letter to Philemon contains our word in verse 6, in which Paul writes of his prayer for Philemon—"That the communication of thy faith may become effectual by the *acknowledging* [*knowledge*—A.S.V.] of every good thing which is in you in Christ Jesus." Our faith in God can only become a power in our lives as we fully understand all that He has given us in Christ, so that we may place our fullest dependence on this ample and gracious provision.

In the Epistle to the Hebrews our word is used in one of the most solemn verses in the whole of the New Testament—Hebrews 10:26: "For if we sin wilfully after that we have received the *knowledge* of the truth, there remaineth no more sacrifice for sins, but a certain fearful looking for of judgment and fiery indignation, which shall devour the adversaries." Knowledge, even though it is a full understanding of the truth which has been heard, and is of a kind that should wield a powerful influence in the life, must wait on the pleasure of the will. It is only too frighteningly possible to know the truth, and to understand its implications, and then by reason of the mysterious gift of free will to say "No" to it. For the man who has seen the true meaning of Calvary, there remains "no more sacrifice for sins" if he deliberately decides to disobey the call of God and to go on living to and for himself.

We are now left with four references to be found in Peter's Second Epistle. Three of them occur in the first few verses of chapter 1: "Grace and peace be multiplied unto you through the *knowledge* of God, and of Jesus our Lord" (verse 2). Right at the beginning of his letter he lays down the only possible basis for peace of heart and true blessing in one's life. This is strengthened in verse 3, which continues—". . . according as His divine power hath given unto us all things that pertain unto life and godliness, through the *knowledge* of Him that hath called us to glory and virtue." Then after careful instruction for the development of the Christian life that has been imparted to us, given in the succeeding verses, and the list of virtues to be earnestly sought after (see Chapter 6), we are told in verse 8: "For if these things be in you, and abound, they make you that ye shall neither be barren nor unfruitful in the *knowledge* of our Lord Jesus Christ."

The final reference is a verse which duplicates the solemn warning of Hebrews 10:26—"For if after they have escaped the pollutions of the world through the *knowledge* of the Lord and Saviour Jesus Christ, they are again entangled therein, and overcome, the latter end is worse with them than the beginning" (2 Peter 2:20).

The knowledge of the truth, and of the Person who is Himself "The Truth," is something to be sought after and valued beyond anything else. This knowledge has power so to transfigure men that they are made anew in the likeness of the Son of

Full Understanding / 71

God. But it is man's will that rules his life: he may see the truth in all its grand attractiveness, the key to all blessedness may be within his grasp, and then he may cast it from him, go out into the outer darkness and be lost eternally. Knowledge brings with it responsibility for deliberate decision, and we need to remember this. It is one thing to know the truth; it is quite another to seek humbly and readily that it may operate in our lives. How carefully we need to handle the Book that brings men into fellowship with the living God!

* * * * *

"The structure of the word 'epignosis' suggests developed knowledge; the New Testament usage tends to connect it with spiritual knowledge. The Colossians had not only heard and, in a natural sense, understood the gospel; they had seen into it with the intuition of grace."

(Bishop Moule, on Colossians 1:6)

* * * * *

"There is a notional knowledge, or, as I may call it, a phantasmatical knowledge of spiritual things—that is whereby a man knows them; but it is by such a kind of light as is in any knowledge and science whatsoever, whereby he knoweth the rationality of things but by images as the fancy delivereth up to the understanding to work upon, by hearsay. But then there is a real knowledge that bringeth down the things into a man's heart. . . . We have a real knowledge of Him through the artifice of the Holy Ghost, and this knowledge now changeth the heart into the same image; therefore no wonder if the apostle here prayeth for spiritual knowledge, and for that alone, for these Ephesians."

(Thomas Goodwin, on Ephesians 1:17)

CHAPTER 8

REFLECTION

AN interesting word which is used in the New Testament in connection with our mental makeup is the Greek word *sunesis* (σύνεσις), which Bullinger defines as: "Intelligence, insight into anything, understanding, cleverness as shown in quickness of apprehension, acuteness, the intelligent penetrating consideration which precedes decision and action. 'Sunesis' is used of reflective thought, 'sophia' (wisdom) of productive thought."

This word appears twice only in the Gospels. In the first case it is used by the scribe to whom the Lord Jesus has just summed up the whole content of the Law in the pungent phrases about loving God with the whole being, and thy "neighbour as thyself." Instead of employing the word "dianoia" (see Chapter 5) in his reply, the scribe says in Mark 12:32–33: "Well, Master, thou hath said the truth: for there is one God; and there is none other but He:

and to love Him with all the heart and with all the *understanding*, and with all the soul, and with all the strength, and to love his neighbour as himself, is more than all whole burnt offerings and sacrifices." He is right! Not only is God to be loved with *all* the powers of our intellect, but with those powers applied in full, penetrating consideration.

The other appearance of our word in the Gospels is in Luke 2:47, where it says of the boy Jesus as He sat in the temple reasoning with the doctors: "And all that heard Him were astonished at His *understanding* and answers." It is hardly surprising that He who was "God manifest in the flesh" should display so remarkable a degree of quickness of apprehension, particularly in regard to matters affecting His Father's kingdom and glory.

Now to turn to Paul's epistles. Our word is used in 1 Corinthians 1:19 where the apostle's theme is the preaching of the cross. In verses 18–19 he says: "For the preaching of the cross is to them that perish foolishness; but unto us which are saved it is the power of God. For it is written, I will destroy the wisdom of the wise, and will bring to nothing the *understanding* of the prudent." The cross is the one basis of all God's dealings with men. He will meet with man only in and through Jesus Christ and Him crucified. Apart from a humble approach to Him in this way ordained by Him, human wisdom, understanding, acuteness—however brilliant—ends in folly. The Church's one weapon for combating sin and darkness is therefore the preaching of the cross; all else just clouds the issue.

Colossians 1:9 forms part of the apostle's prayer for the members of this church (see Chapter 7) and reads—"that ye might be filled with the knowledge of His will in all wisdom and spiritual *understanding*" (and the object of this quickened spiritual perception should be noted) "that ye might walk worthy of the Lord unto all pleasing, being fruitful in every good work, and increasing in the knowledge of God; strengthened with all might, according to His glorious power, unto all patience and longsuffering with joyfulness" (Colossians 1:10–11). True spiritual understanding will manifest itself in radiantly holy living; otherwise you may know that you have to deal with a counterfeit.

Colossians 2:2–3 (see Chapter 6) speaks of the "full assurance of *understanding,* to the acknowledgement of the mystery of God, and of the Father, and of Christ; in whom are hid all the treasures of wisdom and knowledge." A quickened spiritual understanding sees Christ as the source of all good, as the origin of all divine blessing. Here is true insight.

Finally, in 2 Timothy 2:7 Paul is instructing Timothy in the ways of effective ministry, and using simple straightforward illustrations drawn from the life of the soldier, the athlete and the husbandman. He concludes with the exhortation: "Consider what I say; and the Lord give thee *understanding* in all things."

How wonderfully God deals with us men and women! He sets no complicated path of mysticism before us, but asks merely the yielding of all our powers of spirit, mind and body into His hands so that He may teach us Himself, and prolong His days in us to His eternal glory.

CHAPTER 9

PRACTICAL WISDOM

WE have seen in the previous chapter that the Greek word *sophia* (σοφία) is in a sense the complement of the word "sunesis." It is active, whereas "sunesis" is rather reflective. It is used a great many times in the New Testament. According to Liddell and Scott's Lexicon, it means (a) cleverness or skill in handicraft; (b) knowledge of, acquaintance with a thing; (c) skill in matters of common life, sound judgment, intelligence, prudence, practical and political wisdom, and (d) knowledge of a higher kind, as of the sciences, learning, wisdom, philosophy.

At first sight the study of this word seems to present a considerable task, but as you look closer you find that in a number of cases it is either used in parallel passages or is extensively used in a passage in which the object has obviously been to "get across" a certain line of teaching. This fact simplifies our task considerably.

To start with the Gospels, the first use of our word is in Matthew 11:19 (Luke 7:35). Here the Lord Jesus has been contrasting the ministry of John the Baptist with His own, and He comments on the striking differences in these words: "But *wisdom* is justified of her children."

In Matthew 12:42 (Luke 11:31) the Lord Jesus speaks of the *wisdom* of Solomon and the anxiety of the Queen of Sheba to profit by it, and then points out that He is far greater than Solomon and that we need to wait on Him for counsel and instruction.

In Matthew 13:54 (Mark 6:2) we see the amazement with which the people of His own district regarded the Lord Jesus— "Whence hath this man this *wisdom,* and these mighty works?" they ask.

Luke 2:40 and 52 tell us of the divine *wisdom* which rested upon Jesus even in His youth, the wisdom that could not only read the will of God but carry it through. Luke 11:49 speaks of the *wisdom* of God, and Luke 21:15 gives us the first promise that we may by grace become partakers of that wisdom. The Lord Jesus, pointing out to His disciples the opposition and persecution which they must necessarily encounter, gives a clear promise which has been a rock upon which many have happily rested down the ages in their hour of need: "I will give you a mouth and *wisdom*, which all your adversaries shall not be able to gainsay [contradict] nor resist." What a wonderful provision, and how often you and I are beaten back by the opposition of men instead of proving the power of the irresistible wisdom of God!

In the Acts of the Apostles our word is used four times. In the first instance the instructions given by the apostles concerning the appointment of the first deacons, which specifies that they are to be men "of honest report, full of the Holy Ghost and *wisdom*" (Acts 6:3). Were these instructions complied with today, the life of many of our churches would be a great deal healthier! The result of one of the choices then made is seen later in the chapter where Stephen is giving his witness, and it is recorded of him: "they were not able to resist the *wisdom* and the spirit by which he spake" (Acts 6:10). Here is a genuine equipment for service, and how vital it is that we should be endued in this way if our service is to prevail and to be of value to God.

In his defence before the Sanhedrin, Stephen speaks of Moses, in Acts 7:10 and 22, as being filled with wisdom. In the first instance the source of his wisdom is specifically indicated—"God was with him . . . and gave him favour and *wisdom* in the sight of Pharaoh. . . ." In the second instance he speaks of him as being "learned in all the *wisdom* of the Egyptians." It is folly to despise secular knowledge! Moses during his sojourn in Pharaoh's household was being prepared for the leadership which he was later to exercise, and he learned the art of government in an excellent school. In Christian work there is no accumulated knowledge or training that is waste, and we should be careful not to let our wisdom in the practical things of life run to seed. John Newton once declared that if a Christian man was employed as a bootblack, he should be the best bootblack in the town. He was right; men should always be able to rely upon a Christian.

In Romans 11:33 Paul indulges in one of his spontaneous outbursts of praise and adoration: "O the depth of the riches both of the *wisdom* and knowledge of God! how unsearchable are His judgments, and His ways past finding out!" Are you an enthusiast about God and the riches of His wisdom? For myself I think that one of the joys in the Christian life is to be in a position where I cannot do a thing—but have to stand aside and watch God work out His own sovereign purposes. He does things very much better than you and I can!

The First Epistle to the Corinthians has two passages of which wisdom is the theme: chapter 1:14–31 and chapter 2, where our word occurs no less than thirteen times. I think that the easiest way of handling these passages is to outline the main argument contained in them.

In the first chapter a contrast is made between the wisdom of the world and God's wisdom. Paul expresses his fear that any reliance upon the "wisdom of words" in his preaching might mean that the cross of Christ would be emptied of its power. He then goes on to show that what the world calls wisdom is turned to folly by the dealings of God with man in the cross of Christ. Then—is it not truly amazing to compare verse 24 with verse 30 and to discover that Christ is not only "the *wisdom* of God" but that He is "made unto *us* wisdom"! What rest to be able to confess our own utter lack of wisdom, and then to turn and reckon upon the Living Christ to be our wisdom in every circumstance of life!

Chapter 2 extends and amplifies this theme. Here we find voiced the apostle's grand determination not to know anything in his ministry among the Corinthians except "Jesus Christ, and Him crucified."

This is the sole answer to man's need, but its value and significance can only be understood by the direct revelation of God. "But the natural man receiveth not the things of the Spirit of God: for they are foolishness unto him" (verse 14). How long it takes us to grasp this fact, and to turn aside from every other teacher but the Spirit of God, and to wait quietly and humbly upon Him. Only in this way can He impart to us the true wisdom of love which builds up, instead of "puffing up," and makes us teachable and usable instead of being occupied with our own gifts and importance.

In dealing with the controversial question of the gifts of the Spirit, Paul in 1 Corinthians 12:7–8 (see Chapters 2 and 6) insists that all such gifts are given for the profit of all, a condition which should always be kept in mind; and then goes on to specify the very first of these gifts to be "the word of *wisdom*"—the expression of sound, solid, practical judgment.

In 2 Corinthians 1:12 the apostle expresses his joy that he can say that his dealing with the Corinthian church has been in "simplicity" and "godly sincerity" and not—note the contrast—"with fleshly *wisdom*." What a surge forward there would be in the work of God on every front if we who are workers could make the same claim! Fleshly wisdom is a dangerous pitfall in our dealings one with another, but we have the provisions of limitless grace and divine wisdom at our disposal.

In the letter to the Ephesians our word appears three times. Twice, in 1:8 and 3:10, it speaks of God's wisdom. The first reference tells of the "riches of His grace, wherein He hath abounded toward us in all *wisdom* and prudence." The second shows His wisdom towards the Church as being displayed before the "principalities and powers in heavenly places." All created things must marvel at His wisdom, as they will finally bow to His authority (Philippians 2:9–11).

The third use of our word is in Ephesians 1:17 (see Chapter 7). Here we have the other side of the coin! Paul prays that God, who is the Author of all true wisdom, will grant a great boon to these Ephesian Christians—"the spirit of *wisdom* and revelation in the knowledge of Him." What more could they need?

It is interesting to note that in the Epistle to the Colossians, which seems to have been written with the idea of refuting the mental intricacies taught by the Gnostics, our word is used on no less than six occasions, each of them significant. In 1:9, Paul expresses the same longing as he did for the Ephesians, that these believers facing the arguments and contradictions of a sophisticated age might be filled with "the knowledge of His will in all *wisdom* and spiritual understanding." In verse 28 he claims for himself that his is the teaching of genuine wisdom, obviously having in mind the claims of the false teachers. Chapter 2 provides us with a vivid contrast. In verse 3 Christ is held up as the One "in whom are hid all the treasures of *wisdom* and knowledge" (see Chapters 6 and 8)—the one source of wisdom making all others counterfeit. Then in verses 20–23 he speaks of man's fondness for building up a system of outward ordinances, after "the rudiments [basic principles] of the world," fashioned by man's whim, and points out that such things have a veneer of wisdom: "These have indeed an appearance of *wisdom* in promoting rigor of devotion and self-abasement and severity to the body, but they are of no value in checking the indulgence of the flesh" (verse 23, R.S.V.). They who follow such teachings altogether miss the path of true wisdom.

In Colossians 3:16 the Word of God is plainly shown to be the vehicle by which the treasure of wisdom, which is hidden in Christ, is conveyed to the believer. This is followed in 4:5 by an exhortation which seems almost to gather into itself the teaching of the passages already quoted, and points to the fact that it is the life lived by Christians which manifests to the world the reality and wonder of the work of God for those who are in Christ: "Walk in *wisdom* toward them that are without, redeeming the time." True wisdom grasps the truth stressed by a card pinned to my desk:

"Just one life, 'twill soon be past."

Our next reference is James 1:5: "If any of you lack *wisdom*, let him ask of God, that giveth to all men liberally, and upbraideth not; and it shall be given him." Nothing God does for us takes place automatically; wisdom must be sought, and can be found in God alone. The man who seeks elsewhere will seek in vain.

James 3:13–18 is a lovely little passage in which the difference between "the *wisdom* that is from above" and the wisdom that has its outflow from fallen human nature are described with devastating clarity: "Who is a wise man and endued with knowledge among you? Let him shew out of a good conversation [manner of life] his works with meekness of *wisdom*. But if ye have bitter envying and strife in your hearts, glory not, and lie not against the truth. This *wisdom* descendeth not from above, but is earthly, sensual, devilish.

For where envying and strife is, there is confusion and every evil work. But the *wisdom* that is from above is first pure, then peaceable, gentle, and easy to be entreated, full of mercy and good fruits, without partiality and without hypocrisy. And the fruit of righteousness is sown in peace of them that make peace." Surely no comment can make this clearer. What a ground for self-examination such verses make!

In 2 Peter 3:15 Peter bears witness to the wisdom given to his fellow apostle, Paul. True spiritual wisdom always recommends itself to, and is recognized by, those who are led and taught by the same Spirit.

Revelation 5:12 and 7:12 ascribe wisdom to God and to the Lamb; while two other verses—Revelation 13:18 and 17:9 (see Chapter 2)—are verses around which much controversy has raged, which is not our business to touch upon in these pages.

Wisdom is a lovely thing because it has its source in the heart of God and is given to man in Christ, and it must never be debased into the dogmatic self-assurance with which some Christians maintain their views. We need wisdom day by day that we may walk in a way that is pleasing to Him, and as we seek Him it will surely be given.

*   *   *   *   *

"Prudent humility is a quieting grace, and avoideth many storms and tempests which trouble and shake the peace of others. . . . It teacheth us a cautious suspicion of our own understandings, and a just submission to those that are wiser than ourselves. Pride keepeth out wisdom by keeping out the knowledge of our ignorance."

*   *   *   *   *

"Only what's done for Christ will last!" (Richard Baxter)

*   *   *   *   *

"Where wisdom (*sophia*) and knowledge (*gnosis*) have to be distinguished the essential difference appears to be that *sophia* is a moral-mental term, *gnosis* a term purely mental, or rather one which fixes attention on the cognition of truth simply as such. Conceivably, the man of 'knowledge' *may* stop with a mere sight of truth; but the man of 'wisdom' reflects upon it, receives it, in a way affecting character and action. The words 'wise,' 'wisdom' in the Greek, are thus never in Scripture ascribed to other than God or good men, except in an ironical sense."
(Trench, *N.T. Synonyms—2nd Series*)

CHAPTER 10

MIND AND EMOTION

ANOTHER word translated, when used in the plural, by the English word "thoughts" is *enthumēsis* (ἐνθύμησις). Bullinger says of it: "a revolving of the mind (as regards the emotions); revolvings of mind, thought, as being the result of the commotion of the mind, secret motives."

It appears only four times in the New Testament: twice in Matthew's Gospel. In Matthew 9:4 it is used of the thoughts, reflections, revolvings of the mind of the critics of the Lord Jesus as they question His authority to pronounce forgiveness to the man sick of the palsy. (In Luke's account another word, "dialogismos," is used—see Chapter 4). It is also used in Matthew 12:25 to describe the turmoil of thought and emotion which swept over the Pharisees when they were told of the way in which the "Prophet of Galilee" was casting out demons and gaining the confidence of all classes of the populace. In bitter rage they voiced the tumultuous findings of minds dictated by the stress of their emotions: "It is only by Beelzebub, the prince of demons, that this man casts out demons" (R.S.V.) rings out their accusation; and Jesus, knowing the fear and uncertainty that underlay their anger, deigned to reason with them. How easy it is for our thoughts to be dominated by the upsurge of our emotions, and how unsafe it is to rely upon decisions reached and conclusions arrived at under such circumstances.

Hebrews 4:12 shows how, in actual practice, the only answer to such mental commotion is the deliberate recognition of the power of the Word of God. Chapters 3 and 4 of this epistle are devoted to the great theme of the complete rest of heart given by God to those who will trust Him utterly: "For we which have believed do enter into rest" (Hebrews 4:3), is the writer's plain declaration. In verse 10 of this chapter, we are told that the secret of this rest is to turn aside from the inadequacy of our own strivings: "For he that is entered into His rest, he also hath ceased from his own works, as God did from His." Now follows an exhortation! "Let us labour therefore to enter into that rest, lest any man fall after the same example of unbelief." Do you suppose there was any semblance of rest in the hearts of the Pharisees as they strove with might and main to discredit the Christ of God? Does rest ever lie that way? Now, in verse 12, comes the specific for thoughts stirred into a maelstrom by the emotions: "For the word of God is quick [living], and powerful, and sharper than any two-edged sword, piercing even to the dividing asunder of soul and spirit, and of the joints and marrow, and is a discerner [or more literally—a critic] of the *thoughts* and intents of the heart."

Hasty reading, or even mechanical memorization of Scripture, is not enough. The Word must be quietly and deliberately given time and opportunity to criticize and evaluate to us our deepest thoughts, motives and emotions. This might well be termed "the practice of the presence of God." Truly, "all things are naked and opened unto the eyes of Him with whom we have to do" (v.13), and He through His Word reveals to us not only our own wrong thinking and why that leads away from Him, but also His will and the gracious enablement we have through His Holy Spirit that we may do His will.

The last appearance of our word is in Acts 17:29, where this kind of mental activity is referred to as "man's *device*." Paul is dealing with the whole question of idolatry, and the use of our word here would seem to point to the fact that men are liable to fashion idols after the desires of their hearts. How often in heathen religions the natural forces of the earth likely to give plenty and prosperity are deified, because men yearn for security. The Hitler regime in Germany sought to conjure up once again the stern old Norse gods, whose religion was that of violence and conquest. One of the most dangerous mental quirks which can assail men in so-called Christian lands is the invention of a Christ who fits into their own scheme of things, and the consequent rejection of the Lord and Saviour revealed in Scripture and His atoning sacrifice. The type of religion produced in this way can never be stable. It is swayed this way and that, is always seeking something fresh and spectacular, and never goes beneath the surface. It is possible even in the name of evangelism to cater to this, and shut our Lord and Saviour Jesus Christ outside. Not long ago a statement was made in one of our evangelical papers by a well-known leader, to this effect: "*We must give young people what they want.*" This is the way a new mental and emotional idolatry is established, which the Word of God must be allowed to criticize out of existence if His name is to be glorified in our day and generation.

*   *   *   *   *

"If we discover so many '*faults*,' as the geologists call them, in the structure of our minds, it is because our passions have heaved them out of their places and have destroyed their original integrity and order."

(*The Victory of Faith*, by Rev. J. C. Hare)

CHAPTER 11

THE MIND PRODUCES AN ATTITUDE

IN this chapter we propose to deal with two words having the same root, which, in spite of the fact that they only appear in only one or two pasages of the New Testament, do nevertheless throw some real light on our subject.

The first of these words is *phronēma* (φρόνημα). According to the lexicon its meaning is "what one has in mind, what one thinks and feels; hence—mind, thought, feeling, will; knowledge or wisdom, as being the product of the mind." In short, it denotes an *inclination* or *attitude*. The word appears in one chapter only—Romans 8.

In verse 6 of this chapter we are faced with a categorical statement: "The *mind* of the flesh is death; but the *mind* of the Spirit is life and peace" (A.S.V.).* Truth is

---

*This is the most literal translation of this verse.

always grasped by the mind, and a decision of the will is precipitated. If the flesh governs our decision, the result is death; but if, on the other hand, we submit our thinking and the resulting action to the Holy Spirit of God, the upshot is life and peace.

Verse 7 amplifies this statement, and points out the cause of this effect: "Because the carnal *mind* is enmity against God, for it is not subject to the law of God, neither indeed can be." This is a very strong statement! It does not merely say that it is hostile to God, but that *it is enmity against God*. The whole nature and outlook of the mind of the flesh have been so debased by man's fall that it is conformed to the satanic attitude of rebellion, which caused the fall of Lucifer (see Isaiah 14:12–15). It is impossible to bring it into subjection to the law of God because it has no common ground with it. If you and I were to learn to read our reactions and motives in the light of these statements, we would be much quicker to realize our utter dependence on the work of the Holy Spirit in our lives and more likely to find a balanced walk of liberty and fruitfulness in the will of God.

Verse 27 gives us the exact opposite of this verse, and shows the wonderful harmony of the Godhead. "He that searcheth

The Mind Produces an Attitude / 97

the hearts knoweth what is the *mind* of the Spirit, because He maketh intercession for the saints according to the will of God." Here is a revolutionary thought, followed immediately as it is by the verse: "And we know that all things work together for good to them that love God, to them who are the called according to His purpose." While the mind of the flesh can only lead into darkness and loss, the Spirit of God has a clear-cut purpose for each one of us, which is the great High Priest's constant theme of intercession on our behalf. Because of this, all things that are permitted to come into our lives work together for good. If they are difficulties and suffering, they are allowed in order that we may wring from them the blessings God purposes to lavish upon us through them. Once Paul discovered God's will in the matter, even his "thorn in the flesh" was a messenger of blessing and liberty—even though it was also a "messenger of Satan" (see 2 Corinthians 12:7). If, on the other hand, our path is surrounded with joy and prosperity, these are not sent just for our own enjoyment but that they may be means by which the purposes of God may be brought into active operation in our lives, and in the lives of those about us.

The employment of this word "phronema"

four times in this setting would seem to be a deliberate act of the Holy Spirit of God to reinforce a vital lesson, and to bring before us with crystal clarity the ways of life and death. How many failures in Christian work and witness are explained in these verses, and what vistas of possible blessedness are opened up to our vision!

The second of our two words is *phronēsis* (φρόνησις), which means: "wisdom in action—the faculty which applies the principles of wisdom; a minding to do so and so, purpose, intention, practical wisdom, providence." It only appears twice in the New Testament, in Luke 1:17 in the first instance, where the commission of John the Baptist is defined in these words: "He shall go before Him in the spirit and power of Elias [Elijah], to turn the hearts of the fathers to the children, and the disobedient to the *wisdom* of the just; to make ready a people prepared for the Lord." Once more we have disobedience and right thinking and purposing brought into contrast; the disobedience of the natural man must be turned into the practical wisdom of those who depend on Christ and on Him alone for justification, that they may be prepared for the indwelling of God the Holy Spirit.

The other appearance of this word is in

Ephesians 1:8, where the apostle extols the wisdom displayed by God in His plan of salvation. Paul speaks in verse 7 of the "riches of His grace," and then continues: "wherein He hath abounded toward us in all wisdom and *prudence.*" How infinitely wise is God's provision for us in Christ. This fact stands out more and more, the deeper we look into His ways and into the mighty problem of human sin which He has solved. Well may we cry with Paul—"O the depth of the riches both of the wisdom and knowledge of God! how unsearchable are His judgments, and His ways past finding out!" (Romans 11:33).

*   *   *   *   *

"The reason why the mind of the flesh terminates so fatally: it is hostility to God, the Fountain of Life. Alienation from Him is necessarily fatal. It is the flesh which does not (for indeed it cannot) submit itself to God; as the seat of indwelling sin it is in permanent revolt, and those who are *in* it (a stronger expression, yet substantially identically with those who are *after* it, verse 5)—cannot please God."

(*The Expositor's Greek Testament* on Romans 8:7)

CHAPTER 12

THE MIND PRODUCES A PURPOSE

THE word *gnōmē* (γνώμη) is a stronger word than "phronema," and I have sought to bring out the difference between them in these two chapter headings. The one word denotes the breeding of an attitude, the other indicates the hardening of that attitude into a positive purpose, or action, in some given circumstance.

Bullinger defines "gnome" as: "the decision formed, the mind made up, resolution." Its first appearance is in Acts 20:3 where it is translated "he *purposed* to return through Macedonia." Paul was being pursued from place to place by the Judaisers, and had to make a decision as to the course his next journey was to take. He decided, whatever might be the result, to go through Macedonia to do the work that might await him there.

In the First Epistle to the Corinthians it is used three times. It appears in the first place in 1 Corinthians 1:10: "Now I beseech you, brethren, by the name of our Lord Jesus Christ, that ye all speak the same thing, and that there be no divisions among you; but that ye be perfectly joined together in the same mind (see Chapter 2) and in the same *judgment.*" Not only does a unity which will bridge all divisions need to rest on a oneness of mental perception ("nous"), it calls for a sameness of purpose and resolution—for a determination to put the perceived need for unity into action. It is often a lack of this resolve to act together that is the real cause of weakness and disintegration in Christian work. If two Christians were to sit down and examine together the truth they hold in the mind, they might well be astonished at the amount of unanimity that exists between them; but for some reason or other, perhaps because of the emotions of the self-life, it does not prove convenient to act together. That is the rub! And it is the reason why these two words, "nous" and "gnome," are brought together in this verse.

In 1 Corinthians 7, verses 25 and 40, Paul pronounces his "judgment" ("gnome") on the marriage question. He has thought the whole problem through and has arrived at a considered opinion; and this produces a decision, to which he is ready to stand in his dealings with the churches. In exactly the same way, in 2 Corinthians 8:10 he expresses his judgment on the question of giving—a judgment which he implements by making detailed arrangements as to how the offerings for the needy Christians in Judæa should be made.

In Philemon 14, Paul shows a delicacy in his dealings with Philemon reminiscent of his Lord's dealings with him—and with each one of us. He outlines his proposals for Onesimus, reminds Philemon of the debt of gratitude on which he has a right to count, but states he will not dictate to him. "But without thy *mind* [*consent*—R.S.V.] would I do nothing, that thy benefit [good deed] should not be as it were of necessity, but willingly." In God's dealings with us He likewise gives us all the light we need, reveals to us what He has done for us in Christ; but once we know these things, He will not force our will. A modern writer has expressed it this way:

> "Little value is to be placed on the mere possession of truth. It is as valueless as unused food in the body. Many a postmortem has shown an abundance of food in the stomach; and yet there was death! Why? Because the body had not been able to take up the food and convert it into life substance.

So with the spiritual. Angelic post-mortems upon deceased professors of grace may reveal an abundance of truth—resurrections and raptures numbered correctly and in order, the fourfold gospel neatly tabulated, dispensations catalogued and classified, freewill and divine sovereignty checked and balanced—but while they *know* their duty they do not *do* it, and the knowledge without obedience (knowledge that the delinquents fondly supposed to be a through-ticket to glory) was invalid, and their status remains in question even unto this day."

The Christian life is made up of light given and obedience to that light rendered; both these ingredients are necessary. The first alone produces barren intellectual orthodoxy; the second alone, if the light is not carefully checked, can produce fanaticism.

The final appearances of our word are in Revelation 17. First, in verse 13 we are told of the ten kings—"These have one *mind*, and shall give their power and strength unto the beast": they come to a deliberate decision and act upon it. But verse 17 shows the reverse of the coin, and our word is used twice: "For God hath put it in their hearts to fulfil His *will*, and to *agree* [literally—to make one *decision*], and give their kingdom unto the beast, until the words of God shall be fulfilled."

What a note upon which to end! God is on His throne! Never imagine for one instant that either the rulers of the world or Satan, "the god of this world," have the final say as to the turn of events. God is "the One who worketh all things after the counsel of His own will," and the greatest wisdom is just to trust Him and humbly learn to do His will. To pray "Thy will be done on earth as it is done in heaven" is no empty form of words; it is an act of submission, an "amen" to all the will of God. This is the only reasonable attitude for one's life.

* * * * *

"Much of the controversy of the present day arises from failure to recognize the almost infinite variety of the human mind. No two persons look at the same thing in the same way, or give the same version of an incident or a tale. Each colors it with the tint of personal idiosyncrasy, just as each object in nature borrows from sunlight its special hue. Start a dozen devout, deeply taught men to formulate any doctrine of the faith; while each holds the fact, no two will express it in precisely the same way. We must distinguish between *facts* and *views of facts*. Men may not think alike, and yet be of the same mind."

(Dr. F. B. Meyer on 1 Peter 3:8)

CHAPTER 13

CONSCIENCE

RICHARD BAXTER once wrote a book, the title of which may well seem top-heavy to our modern ideas, but it is nevertheless a good title: "On the Mischiefs of Self-ignorance, and the Benefits of Self-acquaintance." This idea of "a knowing with oneself," of "an inward faculty of moral judgment" or "conscience," is conveyed by the Greek word *suneidēsis* (συνείδησις). Bishop Moule writes of this word: "Man has a *conscience*; the knowledge in himself of moral differences." And I have a feeling that this study would be incomplete without mention of it.

It is used on thirty-two occasions in the New Testament, in seven of which Paul is either appealing to the court of his own conscience or expressing the wish that his actions and attitude will commend themselves to the consciences of those to whom he is writing (Acts 23:1 and 24:16; Romans 9:1; 2 Corinthians 1:12, 4:2 and

5:11; 2 Timothy 1:3). It was of tremendous importance to him that this inner voice based on self-acquaintance should witness to the genuineness of his profession; for to follow the guidance of conscience is necessary for healthy Christian living.

One of the very finest books ever written dealing with the psychology of the Christian life is John Bunyan's *Holy War*. In it Bunyan tells us that after Prince Immanuel entered into possession of the redeemed City of Mansoul, he restored Mr. Conscience to his office as Recorder, and in the instructions given to this recommissioned officeholder the following passage occurs: "Wherefore, O Mr. Conscience, although I have made thee a minister and a preacher to the town of Mansoul, yet as to the things which the Lord Secretary [Bunyan's term for the Holy Spirit of God] knoweth, and shall teach to this people, there thou must be His scholar and a learner even as the rest of Mansoul." Through the Scriptures the Spirit of God enlightens the conscience of the born-again Christian, and we do well to heed the admonitions of this preacher whom we house within ourselves.

It is possible to make shipwreck of our lives if this inner faculty of moral judgment is abused. Four references in 1

Timothy show this. In 1 Timothy 1:5 Paul describes the purpose of God's dealings with man in these words: "Now the end [purpose] of the commandment is charity [love] out of a pure heart, and of a good *conscience*, and of faith unfeigned." This describes the normal Christian life. The inner being has been opened up to God, and the conscience now speaks approvingly of our state of heart, mind, and life; and this desirable condition arises from a real, vital faith in God.

The last few verses of this chapter contain a solemn charge to Timothy to "war a good warfare"; and a warning—"holding faith and a good *conscience*; which some having put away concerning faith have made shipwreck" (verse 19). J. B. Phillips' version of these verses makes their meaning crystal clear. He runs verses 18 and 19 into one, and translates as follows: ". . . your ordination, which sent you out to battle for the right, armed only with your faith and a clear *conscience*. Some, alas, have laid these simple weapons contemptuously aside, and as far as their faith is concerned, have run their ships on the rocks." The Christian cannot act aright if out of contact with God, and all contact with God is the outcome of faith. That is the reason why the enemy of our souls continually seeks to turn us aside

110 / The Bible and the Human Mind

from faith to works, knowing that while we are genuinely relying on God we are safe from him, but while our trust is in any measure in ourselves, then we are easy dupes.

1 Timothy 3:9 contains a passage which lays down in no uncertain terms the spiritual qualifications necessary for those holding any office in the visible Church. Here is one of these qualifications—"Holding the mystery of the faith in a pure *conscience*." Then in 1 Timothy 4:2 we again have a warning set before us. Paul here launches out into a description of the activities of false teachers. He points to the source of their errors—"doctrines of devils [demons]" (verse 1). Then he depicts their attitude of mind—"speaking lies in hypocrisy; having their *conscience* seared with a hot iron." Lastly he gives an idea of the subject matter of their teaching, which is summed up by a false and burdensome asceticism which has on the surface some pretense to piety but has nothing in common with the sane, healthy outworkings of lives made new through the gospel.

The Epistle to the Hebrews has two passages containing valuable teaching as to the place of the conscience in the Christian life. Hebrews 9:9 first of all points out that the legal ceremonial of the Law of

Moses was completely unavailing to bring the erring conscience of fallen man into harmony with God. The writer speaks of "gifts and sacrifices . . . that could not make him that did the service perfect as pertaining to the *conscience*." The elaborate ritual of the Jewish worship was merely a picture—"a shadow of good things to come." From all eternity God has purposed to meet man's need in Christ, and the Law only pointed to Him. We are able, therefore, to read on to verse 14, where we find this magnificent proclamation: "How much more shall the blood of Christ, who through the eternal Spirit offered Himself without spot to God, purge your *conscience* from dead works to serve the living God?" A gulf is opened by this verse between two great classes. In the first place there are those who have only a form of religion, whose conscience behaves in a thoroughly unreasonable way. Sometimes it is so quiet that it would seem to be fast asleep, then all of a sudden it is roused into activity and makes a tremendous to-do over some external point of behavior or religion. On the other hand there are those who by the operation of the Holy Spirit have come to realize that there is nothing either in them or in their way of life that can commend them to God. These people find in the death of Christ a restoration of conscience to sanity, and a way of access to God, who now will be their guide in *every* part of life.

Hebrews 10 tells substantially the same story. In verse 2 the inadequacy of the Mosaic Law is again emphasized, showing that if sacrifices offered under the Law had been truly efficacious, the result would have been peace of conscience. Then in verses 21 and 22 we are pointed again to our Lord and Saviour Jesus Christ, our great High Priest, who now presents those for whom He died before the throne of God; and we are summoned to come close to Him, in His name: "Let us draw near with a true heart in full assurance of faith, having our hearts sprinkled from an evil *conscience*. . . ." No man can have any true perspective of his inner condition until he sees himself in his God-ordained relationship to the Saviour, who bore his sins and lives forever on his behalf.

Two chapters in the First Epistle to the Corinthians show us something of the place of conscience in relation to problems that arise in everyday Christian living. In 8:7–13 the Christian is urged to frame his conduct not merely by whether a thing is right or wrong, according to his own judgment, but by considering how any given action will affect his brethren. This surely amplifies the second great commandment: "Thou shalt love thy neighbour as thyself"; therefore anything that might hurt or stumble him is something to be sedulously avoided. To do harm to a fellow Christian by setting an example that might lead him into temptation is a heinous sin in God's sight, and greater far than some petty legal omission on our part.

In chapter 10, verses 23–33, Paul returns to much the same theme. He points out that in the then vexed question of eating meat that has been used in heathen worship it is wise not to inquire about what is set before you at a meal in the house of an acquaintance. But if the fact is pointed out to you that you are about to share in something that has been dedicated at a heathen altar, you must abstain, not so much for your own sake as for the sake of any who may be watching you. You must seek never to act in a way that would reflect badly on the gospel you profess. This is a point upon which we must listen for every whisper of conscience, and ask that we may be quick to discern between right and wrong. It is often in apparently trivial decisions that the biggest issues are at stake.

Finally, Peter in his First Epistle employs our word three times. In 2:18–20 he outlines a great principle of Christian living: "Servants, be subject to your masters with all fear; not only to the good and gentle, but also to the froward [unreasonable]. For this is thankworthy, if a man for *conscience* toward God endure grief, suffering wrongfully. For what glory is it, if, when ye be buffeted for your faults, ye shall take it patiently? but if, when ye do well, and suffer for it, ye take it patiently, this is acceptable with God." One of the great secrets of Christian living is to maintain a genuinely clear conscience towards God, to do right just because it is right, and to face whatever consequences follow quietly and simply. The witness of lives lived in this way is among the most potent recommendations of the validity of the gospel.

Peter again emphasizes this same thought in 1 Peter 3:16. It is a clear conscience that matters. We must be ready to bear witness to our faith (verse 15), but it must be witness backed by the driving force of a good conscience (verse 16) so that even if men speak against you, they may know that what they say is false, and their respect both for you and for the message you bring will be enhanced. The Saviour Himself walked in this path; and although men hounded Him to death, they were forced to admit that they could find no fault in Him.

1 Peter 3:21 provides a fitting conclusion to this section of our study. Baptism has always been a controversial issue between denominations, but this verse lays down with complete clarity that there is no virtue to be found in the rite as such. Baptism itself cleanses none, but "the answer of a good *conscience*" does. Deep down within, when a man has come to know his own need, he also discovers the provision God has made to meet his need in the cross of Christ. So he comes to make his formal act of entry into the ranks of the visible Church, knowing that he has shared in his Saviour's death on Calvary in order that he may also share in the power of His resurrection. In the strength of this knowledge, he is not only able to live a life of loyal church membership but of close fellowship with God. Yes! Bunyan's name for Conscience is a good one—Mr. Recorder; and his function is to teach us how to walk according to the will of God. He provides us with a balance between knowledge and life, and is the prompter of godly behavior based on the teaching of the Holy Spirit through the Word of God.

CHAPTER 14

SOUL AND SPIRIT

ON three occasions in the New Testament the Greek word *psuchē* (ψυχή), meaning "soul," is translated by the English word "mind," which would seem naturally to point to the inclusion of a section dealing briefly with the relationship of soul and spirit in the human makeup.

The word "psuche" is used in the New Testament for either the soul of man or the life with which he is endowed by natural generation. Many writers employ it interchangeably with the Greek word "pneuma" (πνεῦμα)—"spirit." There would seem to be no warrant for this, and if such an interpretation is adopted certain important facts are automatically hidden. In Scripture the word "psuche" is often used in contrast to the word "zōē" (ζωή) which is generally used to express the eternal life which is the gift of God to man in Christ. One passage will serve to show

how clear this contrast is intended to be: "He that loveth his life [psuche] shall lose it; and he that hateth his life [psuche] in this world shall keep it unto life [zoe] eternal" (John 12:25). This teaches me that the "life of nature," to use a favorite term of the old Puritan divines—that life which I have as a human and which is governed by this material world and belongs to time—must be subordinated to the eternal, to that new life which is mine through grace and by faith in the Lord and Saviour Jesus Christ.

In this connection the rare use of the adjective "psuchikos" (ψυχικός)—*animal, as distinguished from spiritual subsistence*—well repays study. The passages in which this word (usually translated "natural" or "sensual") occurs are: 1 Corinthians 2:14 and 15:44, 46; James 3:15 and Jude 19, all of which underline this contrast.

A glance at the verses where "psuche" ("soul") is translated "mind" may well prove to be helpful. The first is Acts 14:2: "But the unbelieving Jews stirred up the Gentiles, and made their *minds* evil affected against the brethren." It is easy by means of carefully worded propaganda to turn the minds of men against those who believe and preach the gospel. That part of man which has its roots in this world—

a world so attractive in all that it has and offers—is peculiarly susceptible to any suggestions which will justify a person in his own eyes to an attitude of indifference and even hostility to the things of God. The secular press, for example, is very quick to fasten on some misdemeanor by a professor of religion and to give it publicity; and there are many who will read such accounts with relish, because they feel that they are justified in saying: "I always knew that religion was a sham." The natural man, because this attitude has penetrated into his thinking, is innately hostile to God and willing to join with those who are against His people.

The second passage is Philippians 1:27: ". . . stand fast in one spirit, with one *mind* striving together for the faith of the gospel." Here is a verse in which a distinction is made between soul and spirit. These men are to follow the dictates of the Spirit—by joining heartily in with those of the same spirit, and coordinating their natural powers also in maintaining the faith of the gospel. It is interesting to compare this verse with Acts 4:32, where the early Christians are described as being "of one heart and of one *soul*," so that even the material possessions of life were shared out as the need arose among them. Our word "psuche" is used here.

The last reference is Hebrews 12:3: "For consider Him . . . lest ye be wearied and faint in your *minds.*" Here the New King James reads: ". . . lest you become weary and discouraged in your *souls.*" The natural powers of man are not able to stand the strain of the Christian warfare. Many a man gives up for this reason (cf. Matthew 13:20–21). It is necessary to enroll in the School of Christ and be educated (this is the primary meaning of the word translated "chastening" in Hebrews 12:5–8, 10–11) so that we may learn the ways of the Spirit and not be dominated by the purely human outlook which is our birthright from Adam. The word rendered "consider" in this verse has much more the force of "reckon on," "calculate on." Only by counting utterly on Christ, and by constant looking away to Him who is able to "save to the uttermost," can a man walk in the path of the will of God. He has no natural powers that can avail him here.

Let us now turn for a brief glance at the contrasting word "spirit" (pneuma). All God's dealings with man in grace are from the inside outwards. Man is spirit, soul and body; and the spirit has rightly been described as the seat of God-consciousness. Scripture bears this out. Romans 8:16 tells us: "The Spirit Himself beareth witness with our *spirit,* that we are children of God" (A.S.V.). We can have no assurance of our acceptance with God by means of a mental grasp of truth; until we have the witness of the Holy Spirit to our *spirit,* doubt and darkness will constantly haunt us.

In John 4:23 the Lord Jesus enunciates a great principle which His dying for man would inaugurate. Up to that time religion had been taught by external ceremonials, and mainly by purely human means. God had given glimpses—mere glimpses—of Himself through these outward things. But with the advent of the Son of God all this was changed. "The hour cometh, and now is, when the true worshippers shall worship the Father in *spirit* and in truth: for the Father seeketh such to worship Him. God is a Spirit: and they that worship Him must worship Him in *spirit* and in truth." This true, spiritual worship means nothing to the natural man, and for this reason Christendom has for so long been a maelstrom of warring sects. There has been so great a concentration on outward forms that men have almost forgotten that the spirit is just as real a part of man as is his body. I recently heard someone discoursing on "the spiritual values of Shakespeare." What they really meant, I suspect, was the aesthetic values. Our terms have become so mixed that many of them have lost their real meaning, and therefore their value.

Paul takes up this thought of spiritual worship and aligns it with prayer: "For God is my witness, whom I serve in [a better translation than "with"] my *spirit* in the gospel of His Son, that without ceasing I make mention of you always in my prayers" (Romans 1:9, margin). Here is the true explanation of praying without ceasing. I have had it said to me: "I cannot spend all my time shut in and on my knees!" True! But deep down in one's spirit there is constant contact with God, and this constitutes the true inwardness of prayer. One of the reasons that the evangelical churches find it so difficult to maintain vital meetings for prayer is that so few church members have any inkling of what this "spirit contact" with God means.

The spirit, again, is the place of our essential union with Christ: "He who is united to the Lord becomes one *spirit* with Him" (1 Corinthians 6:17, R.S.V.). I often meet people who try to "realize" their union with Christ, or endeavor to work out an intellectual system of doctrine by which this union can be effected. The doctrine is clearly written in Scripture but it is spiritually discerned, and is effective in and through the spirit only. Such verses as "Ye are bought with a price: therefore glorify God in your body, and in your *spirit,* which are God's" (1 Corinthians 6:20), and "Having therefore these promises, dearly beloved, let us cleanse ourselves from all filthiness of the flesh and *spirit,* perfecting holiness in the fear of God" (2 Corinthians 7:1) are the natural corollary of this fact. The atoning work of our Lord and Saviour Jesus Christ on the cross was for the whole man, not just part of him.

In Philippians 3:3 Paul defines true believers as those who "worship God in the *spirit,* and rejoice in Christ Jesus, and have no confidence in the flesh." To Timothy he sends the beautiful benediction: "The Lord Jesus Christ be with thy *spirit.* Grace be with you. Amen" (2 Timothy 4:22).

I am deliberately making no attempt to deal exhaustively with this fascinating theme, but only giving a hint to those who care to follow it further, in order that a proper balance may be given to our study as a whole. It is a subject which will well repay careful examination, but one word of warning is necessary. As I once heard it put: "You cannot unscramble an egg!"— the ingredients once mixed cannot again be separated into their component parts. So with man: he is spirit, soul and body, and although we must recognize this fact, and act accordingly, we must always bear in mind that it is not for us to seek to make hard and fast lines as to just where the faculties of one part of us begins and another ends. God uses His Word as a surgeon uses his knife, "piercing even to the dividing asunder of *soul* and *spirit*" (Hebrews 4:12), and we need to watch Him at work within us, and to learn when we are acting simply because our emotions have been stirred or our intellect stimulated, and when, rather, the spirit deep within us is usefully active. This will gradually become a natural part of our daily walk. It will not worry and complicate us, but will bit by bit open our whole being to the gracious influences of the Holy Spirit of God. In this way will the prayer of the apostle be answered: "And the very God of peace sanctify you wholly; and I pray God your whole spirit and soul and body be preserved blameless unto the coming of our Lord Jesus Christ" (1 Thessalonians 5:23).

CHAPTER 15

THE HEART

THERE is one place in the New Testament where one of the words under discussion in the last chapter, the word "psuche," is translated "heart," and that is in Ephesians 6:6. In every other passage the normal word *kardia* (καρδία) is used. Bullinger says of this word: "As the corporeal organ of the body, it is the seat of life, which chiefly and finally participates in all its movements. Also as the seat and center of man's personal life in which the distinctive character of the human manifests itself. Hence the significance of the heart as the starting point of the developments and manifestations of personal life, as well as the organ of their concentration and outgo." Let me illustrate. In Matthew 6:19–20 the Lord Jesus utters His great warning against setting too great a value on earthly things to the exclusion of heavenly things, and in verse 21 gives the reason for the strength of His words: "For where your treasure is, there will your *heart* be also." You will—this is the implication—become completely wedded to the sphere you choose, and the union which has been forged deep down within will have its inevitable outworking in the formation of your character. Your heart will prove to be the final arbiter of your fate. You will either be united to the living God or be rooted in a world doomed to destruction.

I suggested in the opening chapter that the longer I study this subject of the human mind the more passages I have discovered where *mind and heart are linked so closely together* that the reactions of one upon the other can be seen to be of paramount importance to the way that life is lived. It may be that as you have read, you too have been surprised how often the heart turns up in verses in which the mind also is mentioned.

The heart is regarded in Scripture in somewhat the same light as is the root of a tree. From the root the whole tree, including the fruit, draws its life; and the Lord Jesus elaborating this thought said: "Either make the tree good, and his fruit good, or else make the tree corrupt, and his fruit corrupt: for the tree is known by his fruit" (Matthew 12:33). Then He made His application: "O generation of vipers,

The Heart / 127

how can ye, being evil, speak good things? For out of the abundance of the *heart* the mouth speaketh. A good man out of the good treasure of the *heart* bringeth forth good things; and an evil man out of the evil treasure bringeth forth evil things." This harmonizes with Bullinger's definition, and shows the place of the heart in its correct relation to human thinking, which is finally resolved into action and deeds.

Matthew 13:19 depicts a man listening to the preaching of the gospel and states that the word is sown "*in his heart*." This again bears out the contention advanced in an earlier chapter that unbelief is not primarily a thing of the head but of the heart.

In John 12:39–40 the Lord Jesus applies the prophecy of Isaiah 6:10 to the people of His own day: "Therefore they could not believe, because Isaiah again said: 'He has blinded their eyes and hardened their *heart*, lest they should see with their eyes and perceive with their *heart*, and turn for me to heal them'" (R.S.V.). Here it was the inner disposition which was hardened; the result being the blighting, crippling influence of unbelief, until they were firmly convinced in their own minds that their resistance to the Son of God was right, and their condemnation of

Him in accordance with the correct interpretation of their religious beliefs.

Paul in Romans 10:8–10 emphasizes this same harmony between heart and belief as being the basis of our salvation—the pivot upon which all spiritual life turns. "For with the *heart*," he says, "man believeth unto righteousness." The warning of Hebrews 3:12 sounds a solemn note just here: "Take heed, brethren, lest there be in any of you an evil *heart* of unbelief, in departing from the living God"; and in dealing with men I have learned that their problems are not really of the intellect but of the heart. If one reaches the heart, the mind must fall into line; but even when the mind is convinced, if the heart is wrong then all is out of gear. This was the case with Simon the sorcerer (Acts 8:9–24). His thoughts concerning the coming in of the Holy Spirit to possess the lives of true believers in the Lord Jesus Christ were utterly wrong, and the trouble is diagnosed by Peter as having its origin in the heart: "Thou hast neither part nor lot in this matter: for thy *heart* is not right in the sight of God." His thinking was controlled by his desire for his own prominence, and in this way he was led into very great presumption. It is always so! The heart that is consistently set upon its own gain will color the thoughts and bring them into stern captivity to its ambitions and desires.

In two consecutive chapters of the Acts of the Apostles we have verses which throw important light on the teaching of Scripture concerning the heart. In Acts 15:9 Peter is pointing out to the elders of the church in Jerusalem that the gospel is equally for the Gentiles as for the Jews, and says: "And [God] made no distinction between us and them, cleansing their *hearts* by faith" (A.S.V.). This reveals the inner workings of the gospel, which reaches right down to man's heart and purges it of its double-dealing and self-sufficiency so that it may find rest where it is alone possible to find it, in the cross of Christ and His cleansing blood shed there for us. In the next chapter we find Paul in Philippi for the first time. He and his companions visited a group of women, whose habit was to go out of the city to pray by a riverside: "And a certain woman named Lydia, a seller of purple of the city of Thyatira, which worshipped God, heard us: whose *heart* the Lord opened, that she attended unto the things which were spoken of Paul" (Acts 16:14). Here we find God dealing directly through the heart—so that when the truth is presented, it is gladly received and brought to bear upon the outward life.

The third chapter of the Epistle to the Colossians gives us a glimpse of the heart of the Christian: opened by God, purified through union with Christ, and renewed by grace. It is ruled by the peace of God (verse 15), is filled with the music of praise, adoration and thanksgiving (verse 16), and in the service of others, including even our worldly employers, it is dominated by a single purpose: to work so that God may be pleased and glorified. This means that heart and life are linked together in bonds that can never be severed. The analogy of the tree stands: what is seen in the life is the unfailing mirror of the state of the heart.

1 John 3:18–22 has something to say on this score, and once more reveals the harmony that exists between the heart and the outward actions: "My little children, let us not love in word, neither in tongue; but in deed and in truth. And hereby we know that we are of the truth, and shall assure our *hearts* before Him. For if our *heart* condemn us, God is greater than our *heart*, and knoweth all things. Beloved, if our *heart* condemn us not, then have we confidence toward God. And whatsoever we ask, we receive of Him, because we keep His commandments, and do those things that are pleasing in His sight." A man cannot be judged merely by

what he says. If he talks of love, we may expect that love to be worked out in his actions. God tries the heart, and it is according to what He sees there that He judges; and He responds to the undivided heart that overflows in worthy deeds. "Now the purpose of the commandment," writes Paul to Timothy, "is love from a pure *heart*, from a good conscience, and from sincere faith" (1 Timothy 1:5, N.K.J.V.).

It is possible for the heart to be hoodwinked and deceived by outward things, which can and do minister a false sense of security. "If anyone among you thinks he is religious," writes James, "and does not bridle his tongue *but deceives his own heart*, this one's religion is useless" (James 1:26, N.K.J.V.). The word here translated "deceive" occurs only on two other occasions in the New Testament, and these two passages would seem to show the lines along which this heart deception operates. In Ephesians 5:3–5 Paul makes one of his emphatic assertions, that a sinful life and Christian profession can never run in double harness. The new life within the Christian constantly urges him to rebel against the dictates of the old. In verse 6 he then warns: "Let no one *deceive* you with empty words, for because of these things the wrath of God comes upon the sons of disobedience" (N.K.J.V.)

In spite of the unequivocal teaching of Scripture, the old heresy that it is possible to be a Christian and remain contentedly under the dominion of sin crops up continually in various guises. I have been told, "Your standard is too high! You must remember that there are such things as carnal Christians." Here is a point where the razor-edge path lying between truth and error is revealed. It is indeed true that there never has been a Christian who has been free from sin; and it is the sad fact that all of us find ourselves failing and falling into the grievous pitfalls laid for our feet by a peculiarly subtle foe. Again and again we are only too conscious of our carnality. But it is impossible for the true Christian to be satisfied with such a state of things. He is not only humbly penitent when such lapses disgrace his walk with God, but he lays hold on every bit of light from the Word of God—which promises him liberty and offers him triumph over his inward enemies.

When a man is deceived in this way he may be as full of evangelical phraseology as an egg is full of protein, but he will be complacent with himself and hard towards his brethren. His heart is deceived, and he is away from the true grace of God.

The Heart / 133

In 1 Timothy 2:14 our word is used in connection with Eve's deception in Eden: "The woman *being deceived* was in the transgression." Through the senses of sight and hearing there were conveyed to her mind two ideas. In the first place, Satan maligned God as not allowing her to have what she deserved; and in the second place, an attractive vista of new and pleasing experiences was offered her if she would only indulge in this one small act of disobedience. How easy it is for us to be deluded in the very same way! We can be seemingly religious but have utterly wrong thoughts about God and a completely erroneous conception of the values of life lived independently of Him. This is the path to dangerous deception. The heart constantly needs to be faced with the plain truths of the Bible in such a way that they are brought to bear on the whole of our everyday life.

Heart sincerity is the root of all true Christian living. By itself the human heart is "deceitful above all things, and desperately wicked" (Jeremiah 17:9), and it controls our thoughts and our will to its own ends. The heart *cleansed by faith in Christ* becomes His dwelling place by His Spirit (Ephesians 3:17), and bit by bit brings thought, will and outward life under His sway, until at His coming again all is finally conformed to His image.

There comes echoing down the ages the prayer that must find a response deep within all who are His—"Create in me a clean *heart*, O God; and renew a right spirit within me" (Psalm 51:10). Only thus can our lives be brought into harmony with the God who loves us and gave His Son for our salvation.

APPENDIX—LIST OF VERBS
with meanings given in the Authorized Version

NOIEŌ (νοιέω) = *understand*

Matthew 15:17	1 Timothy 1:7
16:9,11	Hebrews 11:3
24:15	Ephesians 3:20–think
Mark 13:14	2 Timothy 2:7–consider
John 12:40	Mark 7:18–perceive
Romans 1:20	8:17
Ephesians 3:4	

SUNEIMI (σύνειμι) = *understand*

Matthew 13:13,14,15, 19,23,51	Luke 18:34
15:10	24:45
16:12	Acts 7:25 (twice)
17:13	28:26,27
Mark 4:12	Romans 3:11
7:14	15:21
8:17,21	Ephesians 5:17
Luke 2:50	Mark 6:52–consider
8:10	2 Corinthians 10:12–are not wise

KATANOEŌ: (κατανοέω) = *consider*

Matthew 7:3	Hebrews 10:24
Luke 12:24,27	Luke 6:41–perceive
Acts 11:6	20:23
Romans 4:19	Acts 7:31,32–behold
Hebrews 3:1	James 1:23,24

DIALOGIZOMAI (διαλογίζομαι) = *reason*

Matthew 16:7,8	Mark 9:33–dispute
21:25	Luke 1:29–cast in her mind
Mark 2:6,8 (twice)	3:15–mused
8:16,17	12:17–think
Luke 5:21,22	John 11:50–consider
20:14	

136 / The Bible and the Human Mind

ENTHUMEOMAI (ενθυμέομαι) = *think*

Matthew 1:20
9:4

with "dia"–Acts 10:19

SOPHIZŌ (σοφίζω) = *become wise*

2 Timothy 3:15–to make wise

2 Peter 1:16–cunningly devised

PHRONEŌ (φρονέω) = *exercise the mind*

Matthew 16:23–savour
Mark 8:33–savour
Acts 28:22–think
Romans 8:5–mind
12:3–(twice) think
12:16–(twice) mind
14:6–(twice) regard
15:5–mind
1 Corinthians 4:6–think
13:11–think
2 Corinthians 13:11–mind

Galatians 5:10–minded
Philippians 1:7–think
2:2–(twice) minded
2:5–let this mind be in you
3:15–(twice) minded
3:16,19–mind
4:2–mind
4:10–(twice) care
Colossians 3:2–set affection on

EPISTAMAI (ἐπίσταμαι) = *know*

Acts 10:28
5:7
8:25
19:15
20:18
22:19
24:10

Acts 26:26
1 Timothy 6:4
Hebrews 11:8
James 4:14
Jude 10
Mark 14:68–understand

GINŌSKŌ (γινώσκω) = *know*

Matthew 1:25
6:3
7:23
9:30
10:26
12:7,15,33
13:11
24:32,33,39
Matthew 24:43

Matthew 25:24
Mark 4:11,13
5:43
6:38
7:24
8:17
9:30
12:12
13:28,29

Appendix / 137

Mark 15:10,45
Luke 1:18,34
2:43
6:44
7:39
8:10,17
9:11
10:22
12:2,39,47,48
16:15
18:34
19:15,42,44
21:20,30,31
24:18,35
John 1:10,48
2:24,25
3:10
4:1,53
5:6,42
7:17,26,27,49,51
8:28,32,52,55
10:14,15,27,38
11:57
12:9
13:7,12,28,35
14:7 (twice)
14:9,17,20,31
15:18
16:3,19
17:3,7,8,23
17:25 (twice)
19:4
21:17
Acts 1:7
2:36
9:24
17:19,20
19:15,35
20:34

Acts 21:24,34
22:14,30
23:28
Romans 1:21
2:18
3:17
6:6
7:1,7
10:19
11:34
1 Corinthians 1:21
2:8,14,16
3:20
4:19
8:2,3
13:9,12
14:7,9
2 Corinthians 2:4,9
3:2
5:16 (twice)
5:21
8:9
13:6
Galatians 3:7
4:9
Ephesians 3:19
5:5
6:22
Philippians 2:19,22
3:10
4:5
Colossians 4:8
1 Thessalonians 3:5
2 Timothy 1:18
2:19
3:1
Hebrews 3:10
8:11
10:34

138 / *The Bible and the Human Mind*

Hebrews 13:23
James 1:3
2:20
5:20
2 Peter 1:20
3:3
1 John 2:3,4,5
2:13 (twice)
2:18,29
3:1,6,19,20,24
4:2,6 (twice)
4:7,8,13,16
5:2,20
2 John 1
Revelation 2:17,23,24
3:3,9
= *perceive*
Matthew 16:8

Matthew 21:45
22:18
Luke 8:46
20:19
John 6:15
Acts 23:6
Galatians 2:9
1 John 3:16
= *understand*
Matthew 26:10
John 8:27,43
10:6
12:16
Acts 8:30
Philippians 1:12
= *have knowledge*
Acts 17:13

EPIGINŌSKŌ (ἐπιγινώσκω) = *know*

Matthew 7:16,20
11:27 (twice)
17:12
Mark 5:30
6:33,54
Luke 1:4
7:37
23:7
24:16,31
Acts 3:10
9:30
12:14
19:34
22:24,29
23:28
25:10
27:39
28:1
Romans 1:32
1 Corinthians 13:12

2 Corinthians 13:5
Colossians 1:6
1 Timothy 4:3
2 Peter 2:21 (twice)
= *acknowledge*:
1 Corinthians 14:37
16:18
2 Corinthians 1:13,14
= *perceive*
Mark 2:8
Luke 1:22
5:22
= *have knowledge*
Matthew 14:35
Acts 4:13
24:8
= *well known*
2 Corinthians 6:9
= *understand*
Acts 24:11

Appendix / 139

The word "oida" is again and again translated in the New Testament as "know." It is the perfect tense of the obsolete root "eido," meaning "I see." It carries the force: "I have seen, and therefore I know." It is used in such places as Romans 6:16 and 7:18, 1 Corinthians 3:16, 5:6 and 6:9, Philippians 4:12, 2 Timothy 1:12, 2 Peter 2:9, Revelation 2:2, and other kindred passages.